HSC
Health & Safety
Commission

General COSHH ACOP
(Control of substances hazardous to health)

and

Carcinogens ACOP
(Control of carcinogenic substances)

and

Biological agents ACOP
(Control of biological agents)

Control of Substances Hazardous to Health Regulations 1999

APPROVED CODES
OF PRACTICE

L5

HSE BOOKS

First published 1995
Second edition 1997
Third edition 1999
Reprinted 1999, 2000

ISBN 0 7176 1670 3

Contents

Introduction

This publication contains three Approved Codes of Practice (ACOPs) entitled *Control of substances hazardous to health* (General ACOP), *Control of carcinogenic substances* (Carcinogens ACOP) and *Control of biological agents* (Biological agents ACOP). The General ACOP applies to all substances, in the circumstances to which the Control of Substances Hazardous to Health Regulations 1999 (SI 1999/437) apply. These Regulations contain the provisions of two sets of earlier Regulations (both now revoked): the Control of Substances Hazardous to Health Regulations 1988; and the Control of Substances Hazardous to Health Regulations 1994.

The main changes made by the 1999 Regulations are:

(a) the definitions of 'carcinogen', 'maximum exposure limit', 'member State' and 'substance hazardous to health' have been amended in regulation 2;

(b) the definitions of 'total inhalable dust' and 'respirable dust' have been added to regulation 2;

(c) the definition of 'registered medical practitioner' has been deleted from regulation 2;

(d) reference to the Personal Protective Equipment at Work Regulations 1992 has been replaced by reference to the Personal Protective Equipment (EC Directive) Regulations 1992 in regulation 7(5);

(e) reference to maximum exposure limit being 'specified in Schedule 1' has been removed from regulation 7(6);

(f) the reference to Schedule 1 has been removed and replaced by 'for which a maximum exposure limit has been approved' in regulation 12(2)(a);

(g) the right of appeal against a medical decision to suspend from work has been extended to Her Majesty's Forces by removing the disapplication previously set out in regulation 17(3);

(h) Schedule 1 - 'List of substances assigned maximum exposure limits' - has been removed from the Regulations and all other Schedules, except Schedule 2, have been renumbered;

(i) some entries have been removed from the former Schedule 8, now Schedule 1 - 'Other substances and processes to which the definition of "carcinogen" relates' - and the entry for used mineral oils has been extended to include non-mineral oils.

Changes involving the General ACOP are:

(a) the deletion of paragraph 3(f) defining a 'substantial' concentration of dust (see paragraph (a) in the section above);

(b) an expanded paragraph 33 relating to control of exposure to hazardous substances not classified as carcinogens;

(c) an amended paragraph 36(a) and (d) relating to substances assigned a maximum exposure limit;

(d) the deletion of paragraph 65 relating to the frequency of examining and testing local exhaust ventilation equipment (see regulation 9(2)(a)), and the renumbering of all subsequent paragraphs;

(e) an amended paragraph 75 relating to monitoring procedures;

(f) the renumbering of all references to Schedules, except to Schedule 2.

Application of the COSHH Regulations to people working under another's direction

Although only the courts can give an authoritative interpretation of law, in considering the application of these regulations and guidance to people working under another's direction, the following should be considered.

If people working under the control and direction of others are treated as self-employed for tax and national insurance purposes they are nevertheless treated as their employees for health and safety purposes. It may therefore be necessary to take appropriate action to protect them. If any doubt exists about who is responsible for the health and safety of a worker this could be clarified and included in the terms of a contract. However, remember, a legal duty under section 3 of the Health and Safety at Work etc Act 1974 (HSW Act) cannot be passed on by means of a contract and there will still be duties towards others under section 3 of HSW Act. If such workers are employed on the basis that they are responsible for their own health and safety, legal advice should be sought before doing so.

Consulting employees and/or safety representatives

Proper consultation with those who do the work is crucial in helping to raise awareness of the importance of health and safety. It can make a significant contribution to creating and maintaining a safe and healthy working environment and an effective health and safety culture. In turn, this can benefit the business by making it more efficient by reducing the number of accidents and the incidents of work-related ill health.

Employers must consult safety representatives appointed by recognised trade unions under the Safety Representatives and Safety Committee Regulations 1977. Employees who are not covered by such representatives must be consulted, either directly, or indirectly through elected representatives of employee safety under the Health and Safety (Consultation with Employees) Regulations 1996. More information on an employer's duties under these Regulations is contained in the free Health and Safety Executive leaflet *Consulting employees on health and safety: A guide to the law* (INDG232).

Health and Safety Commission

Control of substances hazardous to health

Control of Substances Hazardous to Health Regulations 1999

Approved Code of Practice

Contents

General ACOP

Notice of Approval

By virtue of section 16(4) of the Health and Safety at Work etc Act 1974, and with the consent of the Secretary of State for the Environment, Transport and the Regions, the Health and Safety Commission has on 9 March 1999 approved this revised Code of Practice entitled *Control of substances hazardous to health* (1999 edition).

This Code of Practice gives practical guidance on the Control of Substances Hazardous to Health Regulations 1999.

This Code of Practice comes into effect on 25 March 1999 and on that date the edition of the Code of Practice, which came into force on 10 January 1997, shall cease to have effect.

Signed

ROSEMARY BANNER
Secretary to the Health and Safety Commission

9 March 1999

Foreword

This Code has been approved by the Health and Safety Commission and gives advice on how to comply with the law. This Code has a special legal status. If you are prosecuted for breach of health and safety law, and it is proved that you have not followed the relevant provisions of the Code, a court will find you at fault, unless you can show that you have complied with the law in some other way.

Additional Codes of Practice have been approved in respect of certain substances, processes and activities. These give supplementary advice to this General ACOP and should be referred to where relevant.

Regulation 1

Regulation 1

Citation and commencement

These Regulations may be cited as the Control of Substances Hazardous to Health Regulations 1999 and shall come into force on 25 March 1999.

Regulation 2

Regulation

Interpretation

(1) In these Regulations, unless the context otherwise requires -

"the 1974 Act" means the Health and Safety at Work etc. Act 1974;

"the Agreement" means the Agreement on the European Economic Area signed at Oporto on 2nd May 1992 as adjusted by the Protocol signed at Brussels on 17th March 1993[a] *and adopted as respects Great Britain by the European Economic Area Act 1993*[b]*;*

"approved" means approved for the time being in writing;

"approved supply list" has the meaning assigned to it in regulation 4 of the Chemicals (Hazard Information and Packaging for Supply) Regulations 1994[c]*;*

"biological agent" means any micro-organism, cell culture, or human endoparasite, including any which have been genetically modified, which may cause any infection, allergy, toxicity or otherwise create a hazard to human health;

"carcinogen" means -

(a) any substance or preparation which if classified in accordance with the classification provided for by regulation 5 of the Chemicals (Hazard Information and Packaging for Supply) Regulations 1994 would be in the category of danger, carcinogenic (category 1) or carcinogenic (category 2) whether or not the substance or preparation would be required to be classified under those Regulations; or

(b) any substance or preparation -

(i) listed in Schedule 1, or

(ii) arising from a process specified in Schedule 1 which is a substance hazardous to health;

"the Executive" means the Health and Safety Executive;

"fumigation" means an operation in which a substance is released into the atmosphere so as to form a gas to control or kill pests or other undesirable organisms and "fumigate" and "fumigant"shall be construed accordingly;

"maximum exposure limit" for a substance hazardous to health means the maximum exposure limit approved by the Health and Safety Commission for that substance in relation to the specified reference period when calculated by a method approved by the Health and Safety Commission;

"member State" means a State which is a Contracting Party to the Agreement;

2

(a) The Agreement was amended by Decision 7/94 of the EEA Joint Committee of 21st March 1994 (OJ No. L160, 28.6.94, p.1). There are other amendments to the Agreement not relevant to these Regulations.

(b) 1993 c.51.

(c) SI 1994/3247; as amended by SI 1996/1092, 1997/1460, 1998/3106, 1999/197.

Regulation

"micro-organism" means a microbiological entity, cellular or non-cellular, which is capable of replication or of transferring genetic material;

"mine" has the meaning assigned to it by section 180 of the Mines and Quarries Act 1954[(a)]*;*

"occupational exposure standard" for a substance hazardous to health means the standard approved by the Health and Safety Commission for that substance in relation to the specified reference period when calculated by a method approved by the Health and Safety Commission;

"preparation" means a mixture or solution of two or more substances;

"registered dentist" has the meaning assigned to it in section 53(1) of the Dentists Act 1984[(b)]*;*

"respirable dust" means airborne material which is capable of penetrating to the gas exchange region of the lung;

"substance" means any natural or artificial substance whether in solid or liquid form or in the form of a gas or vapour (including micro-organisms);

"substance hazardous to health" means any substance (including any preparation) which is -

(a) a substance which is listed in Part I of the approved supply list as dangerous for supply within the meaning of the Chemicals (Hazard Information and Packaging for Supply) Regulations 1994 and for which an indication of danger specified for the substance in Part V of that list is very toxic, toxic, harmful, corrosive or irritant;

(b) a substance for which the Health and Safety Commission has approved a maximum exposure limit or an occupational exposure standard;

(c) a biological agent;

(d) dust of any kind except dust which is a substance within paragraph (a) or (b) above, when present at a concentration in air equal to or greater than -

(i) 10 mg/m^3, as a time-weighted average over an 8-hour period, of total inhalable dust, or

(ii) 4 mg/m^3, as a time-weighted average over an 8-hour period, of respirable dust;

(e) a substance, not being a substance mentioned in sub-paragraphs (a) to (d) above, which creates a hazard to the health of any person which is comparable with the hazards created by substances mentioned in those sub-paragraphs;

"total inhalable dust" means airborne material which is capable of entering the nose and mouth during breathing and is thereby available for deposition in the respiratory tract.

(2) In these Regulations, any reference to an employee being exposed to a substance hazardous to health is a reference to the exposure of that employee to a substance hazardous to health arising out of or in connection with work which is under the control of his employer.

2

(a) 1954 c.70; section 180 was modified by SI 1974/2013 and 1993/1897.

(b) 1984 c.24.

Regulation

2

(3) In these Regulations, unless the context otherwise requires -

(a) a reference to a numbered regulation or Schedule is a reference to the regulation or Schedule in these Regulations so numbered; and

(b) a reference to a numbered paragraph is a reference to the paragraph so numbered in the regulation or Schedule in which that reference appears.

General ACOP

Substances hazardous to health

1 The Control of Substances Hazardous to Health Regulations (COSHH) apply to substances that have already been classified as being very toxic, toxic, harmful, corrosive, sensitising or irritant under the Chemicals (Hazard Information and Packaging for Supply) Regulations 1994 (as amended) and to those substances which have maximum exposure limits (MELs) or occupational exposure standards (OESs). COSHH also covers other substances that have chronic or delayed effects, for example substances that are carcinogenic, mutagenic or toxic for reproduction. Biological agents are also treated by the Regulations as substances hazardous to health. A substance should be regarded as hazardous to health if it is hazardous in the form in which it occurs in the work activity, whether or not its mode of causing injury to health is known, and whether or not the active constituent has been identified. A substance hazardous to health is not just a single chemical compound but also includes mixtures of compounds, micro-organisms, allergens, etc.

2 COSHH includes special provisions for carcinogens in regulations 7(3) and 7(9). For guidance on risks from carcinogens, employers should read this Code together with the supporting Carcinogens Approved Code of Practice. Medical research on occupational cancer continues to find further substances and processes to which varying degrees of suspicion of causing cancer are attached. It is therefore important to have an active precautionary policy of prevention and control based on up-to-date knowledge of the growing number of substances which are suspected of being carcinogenic but are not yet subject to the special provisions for carcinogens in regulation 7 and the Carcinogens ACOP. The need for prudence applies particularly to substances which have not previously been considered to be hazardous in this way, or perhaps in any way, since they are more likely to have been used without particular care. Prevention is better than cure with all diseases; with occupational cancer and other diseases where the effects of exposure are often irreversible, prevention may be the only cure.

3 In considering whether a substance is hazardous to health, the following additional factors should be taken into account:

(a) different forms of the same substance may present different hazards, eg a solid may present negligible hazard but, when ground into dust of a respirable size, may be very hazardous;

(b) many substances contain impurities which could present a greater hazard than the substance they contaminate, eg crystalline silica is often present in minerals which would otherwise present little or no hazard;

(c) some substances have a fibrous form which may present a potentially serious hazard to health, if the fibres are of a certain size or shape;

2

(d) some substances may be known to cause ill health but the causative agent may not have been identified, eg certain textile dusts causing byssinosis;

General ACOP

(e) combined or sequential exposures to various substances may have additive or synergistic effects;

(f) epidemiological or other data which indicate that a biological agent that does not already appear in the Approved Classification is nevertheless the cause of a hazard to health at work.

4 Sources of information about the hazardous properties of substances include:

(a) information on labels and safety data sheets complying with the Chemicals (Hazard Information and Packaging for Supply) Regulations 1994 (as amended), or from classifying the substances by applying the criteria in those Regulations;

(b) information provided by the manufacturer or supplier of the substance under section 6 of the Health and Safety at Work etc Act 1974 (amended by the Consumer Protection Act 1987);

(c) guidance material published by the Health and Safety Executive (HSE) or other authoritative bodies;

(d) experience obtained and information gathered as a result of previous use of the substance or similar substances;

(e) technical reference sources (textbooks, scientific/technical papers, trade journals, etc);

(f) professional institutions, trade associations, trade unions and specialist consultancy services.

2

Regulation 3

Duties under these Regulations

Regulation

(1) Where any duty is placed by these Regulations on an employer in respect of his employees, he shall, so far as is reasonably practicable, be under a like duty in respect of any other person, whether at work or not, who may be affected by the work carried on by the employer except that the duties of the employer -

(a) under regulation 11 (health surveillance) shall not extend to persons who are not his employees; and

(b) under regulations 10 and 12(1) and (2) (which relate respectively to monitoring and information, training etc) shall not extend to persons who are not his employees, unless those persons are on the premises where the work is being carried on.

(2) These Regulations shall apply to a self-employed person as they apply to an employer and an employee and as if that self-employed person were both an employer and employee, except that regulations 10 and 11 shall not apply to a self-employed person.

(3) The duties imposed by these Regulations shall not extend to the master or crew of a sea-going ship or to the employer of such persons in relation to the normal shipboard activities of a ship's crew under the direction of the master.

3

General ACOP

3

5 These Regulations place specific duties on employers, self-employed people and employees. The table at the top of page 5 summarises the scope of the employer's duties in respect of employees and other people.

Duty of employer relating to:	*Duty for the protection of:*		
	Employees	*Other people at the premises*	*Other people likely to be affected by work*
Assessment (regulation 6)	Yes	SFRP	SFRP
Prevention or control of exposure (regulation 7)	Yes	SFRP	SFRP
Use of control measures and maintenance, examination and test of control measures (regulations 8 and 9)	Yes	SFRP	SFRP
Monitoring exposure at workplace (regulation 10)	Yes, where requisite	SFRP	No
Health surveillance (regulation 11)	Yes, where appropriate	No	No
Information, training, etc (regulation 12)	Yes	SFRP	No

SFRP = So far as is reasonably practicable.

6 Contractors, subcontractors and self-employed people all have the duties of employers under the Regulations. Where the employee of one employer works at another employer's premises, both employers will have duties under the Regulations. Each employer will owe these duties to his own employees and, as far as is reasonably practicable, to the employees of the other, and so in most such cases co-operation and collaboration between employers will be necessary to ensure that these duties are fulfilled and this may entail a decision as to who is to undertake them. For example, it will usually be appropriate if the employer having control of the work undertakes exposure monitoring. Also, the obligation to train rests with the actual employer of the person carrying out the work, but the occupier of the premises who requires the work to be done must provide sufficient information about the specific circumstances of the workplace, the risks, etc to enable the training to be suitable and sufficient; the occupier will equally need to know about any risks to health created by the work being carried out.

7 Employers in charge of premises should also take steps to ensure, so far as is reasonably practicable, that visiting members of the emergency services (in particular, firefighters) are made aware of any substances on the premises which offer a significant risk to their health.

3

8 Employees should co-operate with their employers so far as this is necessary to enable an employer to meet the employer's obligations. Regulation 8(2) requires employees to make full and proper use of any control measures, etc and to report defects. Regulation 11(9) of these Regulations requires employees to attend for medical examinations, where appropriate, and give an employment medical adviser or appointed doctor such information about their health as may reasonably be required.

Regulation 4

Prohibitions relating to certain substances

Regulation

(1) Those substances described in Column 1 of Schedule 2 are prohibited to the extent set out in the corresponding entry in Column 2 of that Schedule.

(2) The importation into the United Kingdom, other than from another member State, of the following substances and articles is prohibited, namely -

(a) 2-naphthylamine, benzidine, 4-aminodiphenyl, 4-nitrodiphenyl, their salts and any substance containing any of those compounds in a total concentration equal to or greater than 0.1 per cent. by mass;

(b) matches made with white phosphorus,

and any contravention of this paragraph shall be punishable under the Customs and Excise Management Act 1979[(a)] and not as a contravention of a health and safety regulation.

(3) A person shall not supply during the course of or for use at work any substance or article specified in paragraph (2).

(4) A person shall not supply during the course of or for use at work, benzene or any substance containing benzene unless its intended use is not prohibited by item 11 of Schedule 2.

4

(a) 1979 c.2.

General ACOP

4

9 Provision has been made in regulation 14 for the Health and Safety Executive to grant exemptions from these prohibitions, but only where it can be satisfied that the health of persons will not be prejudiced as a consequence.

Regulation 5

Application of regulations 6 to 12

Regulation

(1) Regulations 6 to 12 shall have effect with a view to protecting persons against risks to their health, whether immediate or delayed, arising from exposure to substances hazardous to health except -

(a) where and to the extent that the following Regulations apply, namely -

(i) the Control of Lead at Work Regulations 1998[(a)];

(ii) the Control of Asbestos at Work Regulations 1987[(b)];

(b) where the substance is hazardous to health solely by virtue of its radioactive, explosive or flammable properties, or solely because it is at a high or low temperature or a high pressure;

(c) where the risk to health is a risk to the health of a person to whom the substance is administered in the course of his medical treatment;

(d) where the substance hazardous to health is total inhalable dust which is below ground in any mine of coal.

(2) In paragraph 1(c) "medical treatment" means medical or dental examination or treatment which is conducted by, or under the direction of, a registered medical practitioner or registered dentist and includes any such examination, treatment or administration of any substance conducted for the purpose of research.

5

(a) SI 1998/543.
(b) SI 1987/2115, amended by SI 1992/3068, SI 1998/3235.

Regulation

5

(3) Nothing in these Regulations shall prejudice any requirement imposed by or under any enactment relating to public health or the protection of the environment.

General ACOP

10 The circumstances in which regulations 6-12 apply include those where the hazard to health is caused by exposure to a biological agent which arises out of, or in connection with, work which is under the control of the employer, but in their application to hazards associated with biological agents they are modified and supplemented by Schedule 3. As specified in regulation 2(2), COSHH covers only the cases where exposure risks are work-associated, not those where it has no direct connection with the work being done. For example, COSHH does not cover exposures such as respiratory infections caught from other employees. Schedule 3 draws a further distinction between exposure where there is a deliberate intention to use or work with a biological agent and exposure which, while still work-associated, is incidental to the main purpose of the activity. (See also paragraph 10 of the Biological Agents ACOP.)

11 Regulation 5(3) ensures that COSHH does not become the 'superior instrument' displacing existing public health and environmental law, such as the Public Health Acts and Food Hygiene (General) Regulations 1970, designed to protect, for example, the consumer of food.

5

Regulation 6

Assessment of health risks created by work involving substances hazardous to health

Regulation

(1) An employer shall not carry on any work which is liable to expose any employees to any substance hazardous to health unless he has made a suitable and sufficient assessment of the risks created by that work to the health of those employees and of the steps that need to be taken to meet the requirements of these Regulations.

(2) The assessment required by paragraph (1) shall be reviewed regularly and forthwith if -

(a) there is reason to suspect that the assessment is no longer valid; or

(b) there has been a significant change in the work to which the assessment relates,

and, where as a result of the review, changes in the assessment are required, those changes shall be made.

6

General ACOP

12 The purpose of an assessment is to enable a valid decision to be made about measures necessary to control substances hazardous to health arising from any work. It also enables the employer to demonstrate readily, both to himself and other people, that all the factors pertinent to the work have been considered, and that an informed and valid judgement has been reached about the risks, the steps which need to be taken to achieve and maintain adequate control, the need for monitoring exposure at the workplace and the need for health surveillance.

13 Whoever carries out the assessment should be competent to do so in accordance with regulation 12(3).

Suitable and sufficient

6

14 A suitable and sufficient assessment should include:

(a) an assessment of the risks to health;

(b) consideration of the practicability of preventing exposure to hazardous substances;

(c) the steps which need to be taken to achieve adequate control of exposure where prevention is not reasonably practicable, in accordance with regulation 7; and

(d) identification of other action necessary to comply with regulations 8-12.

15 An assessment of the risks created by any work should involve:

(a) consideration of:

(i) which substances or types of substance (including biological agents) employees are liable to be exposed to (taking into account the consequences of possible failure of any control measure provided to meet the requirements of regulation 7);

(ii) what effects those substances can have on the body;

(iii) where the substances are likely to be present and in what form;

(iv) the ways in which and the extent to which any groups of employees or other people could potentially be exposed, taking into account the nature of the work and process, and any reasonably foreseeable deterioration in, or failure of, any control measure provided for the purposes of regulation 7;

(b) an estimate of exposure, taking into account engineering measures and systems of work currently employed for controlling potential exposure;

(c) where valid standards exist, representing adequate control, comparison of the estimate with those standards.

16 If comparison shows that control is likely to be inadequate or become inadequate, then the assessment should go on to determine the steps, or, in the case of existing work, the further steps which need to be taken to obtain and sustain adequate control. As required by regulation 7, personal protective equipment should only be considered as a method of control after all other measures have been taken so far as is reasonably practicable.

17 An assessment can be considered sufficient and suitable if the detail and expertise with which it is carried out are commensurate with the nature and degree of risk arising from the work, as well as the complexity and variability of the process.

18 The amount of detailed work involved in carrying out a sufficient and suitable assessment will vary and will depend on the extent to which:

(a) the degree and nature of the risk and conclusions about the adequacy of proposed or existing control measures are immediately obvious;

(b) knowledge has already been gained as a result of previous experience;

(c) existing records are valid, concerning the nature of the substances involved, the numbers and categories of employees potentially exposed, their work activities, the results of exposure experienced hitherto and the suitability of existing methods of control.

19 In some circumstances it will only be necessary to read suppliers' information sheets to conclude that existing practices are sufficient to ensure adequate control of exposure. In others it may be necessary to read HSE guidance notes, manufacturers' standards, technical papers or trade literature to estimate the likely exposure and before deciding what control measures should be applied.

20 The assessment may necessitate the carrying out of atmospheric sampling and measurement to determine exposure, particularly where operations are complex or specialised and the substances involved have an occupational exposure limit.

Provision of information

21 In the simplest and most obvious cases which can be easily repeated and explained at any time, an assessment need not be recorded. But in most cases, to be suitable and sufficient, it will need to be recorded and kept readily accessible to ensure continuity and accuracy of knowledge among all those who may need to know the results.

22 Employees or their representatives at the place of work should be informed of the results of the assessment in accordance with regulation 12(1).

Review of assessment

23 The assessment should be reviewed regularly and in any case whenever there is any evidence to suspect that it is no longer valid or where there has been a significant change in the work to which the assessment relates.

24 The assessment may be shown to be no longer valid because of, for example:

(a) the results of periodic thorough examinations and tests of engineering controls (regulation 9);

(b) the results of monitoring exposure at the workplace (regulation 10);

(c) the results of health surveillance (regulation 11), or a confirmed case of occupationally-induced disease;

(d) new information on health risks.

25 A significant change in the work may be:

(a) in the substances used or their source;

(b) plant modification, including engineering controls;

(c) in the process or methods of work;

(d) in the volume or rate of production.

26 Arrangements should be made to ensure that the assessment is reviewed regularly. The assessment should include a decision, and where the assessment is written, a statement, specifying the maximum period which should elapse between the date of the initial assessment and the date of the first review, and then between successive reviews. The length of the period chosen will depend on the nature of the risk, the work and a judgement on the likelihood of changes occurring, but in any case the assessment should be reviewed at least every five years.

6

General ACOP

6

27 Reviews triggered by these arrangements will provide the opportunity to reconsider the practicability of preventing exposure to hazardous substances by changes to the process or by the use of less hazardous substances. This might now be practicable because of technological changes, or because of changes in the relationship between costs of substances, equipment used and control measures, since the last assessment. Similarly, control measures should be re-examined to assess the feasibility of further improvement; for example, where substances with MELs are involved, do the controls really reduce exposure as far as is reasonably practicable, or merely below the MELs?

Regulation 7

Prevention or control of exposure to substances hazardous to health

Regulation

7

(1) Every employer shall ensure that the exposure of his employees to substances hazardous to health is either prevented or, where this is not reasonably practicable, adequately controlled.

(2) So far as is reasonably practicable, the prevention or adequate control of exposure of employees to a substance hazardous to health, except to a carcinogen or a biological agent, shall be secured by measures other than the provision of personal protective equipment.

(3) Without prejudice to the generality of paragraph (1), where the assessment made under regulation 6 shows that it is not reasonably practicable to prevent exposure to a carcinogen by using an alternative substance or process, the employer shall apply all the following measures, namely -

(a) the total enclosure of the process and handling systems unless this is not reasonably practicable;

(b) the use of plant, processes and systems of work which minimise the generation of, or suppress and contain, spills, leaks, dust, fumes and vapours of carcinogens;

(c) the limitation of the quantities of a carcinogen at the place of work;

(d) the keeping of the number of persons who might be exposed to a carcinogen to a minimum;

(e) the prohibition of eating, drinking and smoking in areas that may be contaminated by carcinogens;

(f) the provision of hygiene measures including adequate washing facilities and regular cleaning of walls and surfaces;

(g) the designation of those areas and installations which may be contaminated by carcinogens, and the use of suitable and sufficient warning signs; and

(h) the safe storage, handling and disposal of carcinogens and use of closed and clearly labelled containers.

(4) Where the measures taken in accordance with paragraph (2) or (3), as the case may be, do not prevent, or provide adequate control of, exposure to substances hazardous to health to which those paragraphs apply, then, in addition to taking those measures, the employer shall provide those employees with such suitable personal protective equipment as will adequately control their exposure to those substances.

Regulation

(5) Any personal protective equipment provided by an employer in pursuance of this regulation shall comply with any provision in the Personal Protective Equipment (EC Directive) Regulations 1992[(a)] which is applicable to that item of personal protective equipment.

(6) Where there is exposure to a substance for which a maximum exposure limit has been approved, the control of exposure shall, so far as the inhalation of that substance is concerned, only be treated as being adequate if the level of exposure is reduced so far as is reasonably practicable and in any case below the maximum exposure limit.

(7) Without prejudice to the generality of paragraph (1), where there is exposure to a substance for which an occupational exposure standard has been approved, the control of exposure shall, so far as the inhalation of that substance is concerned, be treated as being adequate if -

(a) that occupational exposure standard is not exceeded; or

(b) where that occupational exposure standard is exceeded, the employer identifies the reasons for the standard being exceeded and takes appropriate action to remedy the situation as soon as is reasonably practicable.

(8) Where respiratory protective equipment is provided in pursuance of this regulation, then it shall -

(a) be suitable for the purpose; and

(b) comply with paragraph (5) or, where no requirement is imposed by virtue of that paragraph, be of a type approved or shall conform to a standard approved, in either case, by the Executive.

(9) In the event of the failure of a control measure which might result in the escape of carcinogens into the workplace, the employer shall ensure that -

(a) only those persons who are responsible for the carrying out of repairs and other necessary work are permitted in the affected area and they are provided with suitable respiratory protective equipment and protective clothing; and

(b) employees and other persons who may be affected are informed of the failure forthwith.

(10) Schedule 3 of these Regulations shall have effect in relation to biological agents.

(11) In this regulation, "adequate" means adequate having regard only to the nature of the substance and the nature and degree of exposure to substances hazardous to health and "adequately" shall be construed accordingly.

7

(a) SI 1992/3139.

General ACOP

28 Regulation 7(1) sets out the general duty: the employer must ensure that the exposure of employees to substances hazardous to health by **any** route (eg inhalation, ingestion, absorption through the skin or contact with the skin) is either prevented or, where this is not reasonably practicable, adequately controlled.

Meaning of adequate control

29 Adequate control will have been achieved if the standards set out in paragraphs 36 to 39 have been met.

7

Prevention of exposure

30 For all hazardous substances in the workplace, the employer must give first priority to trying to prevent exposure. This might be achieved by:

(a) changing the method of work so that the operation giving rise to the exposure is no longer necessary;

(b) modifying the process to eliminate production of a hazardous by-product or waste product; or

(c) where a hazardous substance is used intentionally, substitution by a new substance or different form of the same substance which, in the circumstances of the work, presents no risk or less risk to health.

31 It is important when considering substituting one substance for another to take into account all the potentially harmful properties of any proposed replacement and to balance any new risks they might present against the possible benefits. For example, in seeking a less toxic substitute chemical for a process, the choice of one with lower toxicity but higher flammability might increase the overall risk if the process has an intrinsic fire risk.

Prevention or control of exposure to carcinogens

32 Regulations 7(3) and 7(9) contain special provisions for prevention or control of exposure to carcinogens. These provisions state that, for carcinogens, if complete prevention is not reasonably practicable, the control measures listed in regulation 7(3)(a)-(h) **must all be taken**. This means that whether or not it is reasonably practicable to enclose totally the process and handling systems in accordance with regulation 7(3)(a), all the other measures in 7(3)(b)-(h) are still required. Regulation 7(9) deals with failures of control which might result in the escape of carcinogens into the workplace, limiting access to the affected area to those carrying out repairs and other necessary work. This would include any essential attendance by the emergency services.

Control of exposure to hazardous substances not classified as carcinogens

33 For hazardous substances not classified as carcinogens, where prevention of exposure is not reasonably practicable, adequate control of exposure should be achieved by measures other than personal protective equipment, so far as is reasonably practicable, in the light of the degree of exposure, circumstances of use of the substance, informed knowledge about its hazards and current technical developments. In seeking to achieve adequate control, employers may find it helpful to refer to *COSHH essentials: Easy steps to control hazardous substances.** The guidance can provide a contribution to a risk assessment, as required by regulation 6, and help in the selection and use of suitable control measures. Any environmental legislative requirements must also be taken into account. Control measures could be any combination of the following:

(a) totally enclosed process and handling systems;

(b) plant or processes or systems of work which minimise generation of, or suppress or contain, the hazardous dust, fume, biological agent, etc and which limit the area of contamination in the event of spills and leaks;

* See HSE publication, *COSHH essentials: Easy steps to control chemicals*, HSE Books ISBN 0 7176 2421 8 (to be published in May 1999).

(c) partial enclosure, with local exhaust ventilation;

(d) local exhaust ventilation;

(e) sufficient general ventilation;

(f) reduction of numbers of employees exposed and exclusion of non-essential access;

(g) reduction in the period of exposure for employees;

(h) regular cleaning of contamination from, or disinfection of, walls, surfaces, etc;

(i) provision of means for safe storage and disposal of substances hazardous to health;

(j) prohibition of eating, drinking, smoking, etc in contaminated areas;

(k) provision of adequate facilities for washing, changing and storage of clothing, including arrangements for laundering contaminated clothing.

Review of control measures

34 In existing work situations, the present control measures should be carefully reviewed, and improved, extended or replaced as necessary to be capable of achieving, and sustaining, adequate control.

Emergencies

35 If, in spite of the above control measures, leaks, spills or uncontrolled releases of a hazardous substance could still occur, means should be available for limiting the extent of risks to health and for regaining adequate control as soon as possible. The means should include, where appropriate, established emergency procedures, safe disposal of the substance and sufficient suitable personal protective equipment to enable the source of the release to be safely identified and repairs to be made. All persons not concerned with the emergency action should be excluded from the area of contamination.

Adequate control — exposure by inhalation

Substances assigned a maximum exposure limit (MEL)

36(a) Regulation 7(6) requires that control of exposure to any substance for which a maximum exposure limit (MEL) has been approved shall only be treated as adequate if the exposure is reduced so far as is reasonably practicable and, in any case, below the MEL. The MEL is the maximum concentration of an airborne substance, averaged over a reference period, to which employees may be exposed by inhalation under any circumstances. The list of MELs, together with the appropriate reference periods and the approved methods for averaging over these specified reference periods is published in HSE's publication EH 40 *Occupational exposure limits.**

(b) Regulation 7(6), when read in conjunction with regulation 16, imposes a duty on the employer to take all reasonable precautions and to exercise all due diligence to achieve those requirements.

(c) In the case of substances with an 8-hour long-term reference period, unless the assessment carried out in accordance with regulation 6 shows

7

* HSE guidance booklet *Occupational exposure limits* EH40/99 HSE Books 1999 ISBN 0 7176 1660 6.

that the level of exposure is most unlikely ever to exceed the MEL, to comply with this duty the employer should undertake a programme of monitoring in accordance with regulation 10 so that he can show (if it is the case) that the MEL is not normally exceeded, ie that an occasional result above the MEL is without real significance and is not indicative of a failure to maintain adequate control.

(d) Some substances for which MELs have been approved have been assigned short-term MELs (eg 15-minute reference period). These substances give rise to acute effects and the purpose of limits of this kind is to render insignificant the risks to health resulting from brief exposures to the substance. For this reason, **short-term exposure limits should never be exceeded.**

(e) The extent to which it is required to reduce exposure further below the MEL will depend on the nature of the risk presented by the substance in question, weighed against the cost and the effort involved in taking measures to reduce the risk.

Substances assigned an occupational exposure standard (OES)

37(a) OESs are approved by the Health and Safety Commission (HSC) and are contained in the List of Approved OESs. The approval by HSC limits the application of the OESs to people at work and to conditions where the atmospheric pressure is normal (between 900 and 1100 millibars). For a substance which has been assigned an OES, exposure by inhalation should be reduced to that standard. However, if exposure by inhalation exceeds the OES, then control will still be deemed to be adequate, provided that the employer has identified why the OES has been exceeded and is taking appropriate steps to comply with the OES as soon as is reasonably practicable. In such a case the employer's objective must be to reduce exposure to the OES; however, the final achievement of this objective may take some time. Factors which need to be considered in determining the urgency of the necessary action include the extent and cost of the required measures in relation to the nature and degree of exposure involved.

(b) For a single substance, control to the OES, or below it, can always be regarded as adequate control of that substance for the purposes of these Regulations, so far as exposure to inhalation is concerned.

(c) HSE's publication EH 40 *Occupational exposure limits* (see page 13) includes the lists of MELs and OESs, the approved methods for averaging over the specified reference periods, an explanation of the terms 'respirable' and 'total inhalable', and related material.

Inhaled substances not assigned MELs or OESs

38 The absence of a substance from the lists of MELs and OESs does not indicate that it is safe. In these cases, exposure should be controlled to a level to which nearly all the working population could be exposed, day after day at work, without adverse effects on health. As part of the assessment required under regulation 6, employers should determine their own working practices, and in-house standards for control. These requirements will also apply in situations where the substance has an OES, but it is not applicable for the reasons described in the preceding paragraph. In some cases there may be sufficient information to set a self-imposed working standard, eg from manufacturers and suppliers of the substance, from publications of industry associations, occupational medicine and hygiene journals.

7

Adequate control - exposure by routes other than inhalation

39 Exposure to any substance which can be hazardous by ingestion, absorption through the skin or mucous membranes, or contact with the skin or mucous membranes (eg microbial infection, dermatitis and chemical burns), should be controlled to a standard such that nearly all the population could be exposed repeatedly without any adverse health effect. Information about appropriate standards of control may be sought from the same types of source, as in the preceding paragraph; aspects to consider include the design and construction of the plant, the cleanliness of the workplace, personal hygiene practices, the layout of the workplace and equipment, working practices and use of personal protective equipment (see also paragraphs 46-49).

Measuring levels of exposure

40 Compliance with occupational exposure limits may be demonstrated by measuring and recording the exposure of employees according to the principles set out in the HSE publication *Monitoring strategies for toxic substances.** This gives detailed advice on the sampling strategies which are suitable to measure exposure, together with practical guidance on the interpretation of the results in relation to occupational exposure limits.

Situations where personal protective equipment may be necessary

41 Examples of situations where the use of suitable personal protective equipment may be necessary include:

(a) where it is at present not technically feasible to achieve adequate control of exposure by process, operational and engineering measures alone. In these cases, exposure should be reduced so far as is reasonably practicable by these measures, and then, in addition, suitable personal protective equipment should be used to secure adequate control;

(b) where a new or revised assessment indicates that personal protective equipment is necessary to safeguard health until such time as adequate control is achieved by other means;

(c) where urgent action is required, eg because of plant failure, the only practicable solution in the time available may be the provision and use of personal protective equipment; and

(d) during routine maintenance operations. Although exposure occurs regularly during such work, the infrequency and small number of people involved may make process control measures unwarranted.

However, in determining the extent to which it would not be reasonably practicable to introduce these other measures, the limitations of personal protective equipment and the costs and practical difficulties of ensuring its continued correct use and effectiveness should be carefully evaluated in the context of the particular work situation and the nature and degree of exposure.

Standards for personal protective equipment

42 The term 'personal protective equipment' includes respiratory protective equipment, protective clothing, footwear and equipment to protect the eyes. Throughout the period during which personal protective equipment is

7

* See HSE guidance booklet *Monitoring strategies for toxic substances* HSG173, HSE Books 1997 ISBN 0 7176 1411 5.

necessary it should adequately control exposure to those hazardous substances to which the wearer is exposed or is liable to be exposed.

43 Selection of protective clothing should take into account:

(a) the ability of the material from which it is made to resist penetration by the substance concerned;

(b) the adequacy of the design of the clothing, and whether it is suitable for the intended use;

(c) the environment in which it will be worn;

(d) in the case of dust, the dust release characteristics of the material.

44 Manufacturers of personal protective equipment will have to ensure that their products comply with the the requirements of Council Directive 89/686/EEC, which is implemented in Great Britain by the Personal Protective Equipment (EC Directive) Regulations 1992.

45 Where respiratory protective equipment is provided, it must be capable of adequately controlling exposure and be suitable for the purpose. To be regarded as suitable, respiratory protective equipment must be correctly selected and used. It must be correctly matched to the job and the wearer.

Facilities for washing, clothing accommodation, eating, drinking

46 Adequate washing facilities should be provided in order to enable persons exposed to meet a standard of personal hygiene consistent with the adequate control of exposure and the need to avoid the spread of substances hazardous to health. The washing facilities should be conveniently accessible but situated so that they do not themselves become contaminated; the type of facilities provided should be related to the nature and degree of exposure. Employers should be aware that they may also have duties under the Workplace (Health, Safety and Welfare) Regulations 1992 in relation to the provision of washing facilities.

47 Clothing accommodation should be provided when personal protective clothing is used or when there is a risk of contamination of outdoor clothing by substances hazardous to health. The changing facilities should be located and designed so as to prevent the spread of contamination from protective clothing to personal clothing and from one facility to another. Employers should be aware that they may also have duties under the Workplace (Health, Safety and Welfare) Regulations 1992 in relation to the provision of changing facilities.

48 In order to reduce the risk of ingestion of substances hazardous to health, people should not eat, chew, drink or smoke in places which are contaminated by such substances arising from the work activities. Places in which contamination is likely to be present include any area where the adequate control of exposure can only be achieved by employees wearing personal protective equipment.

49 Wherever it is necessary to prohibit eating or drinking, suitable facilities should be set aside for these activities to be carried out in an uncontaminated area. This is also a requirement of the Workplace (Health, Safety and Welfare) Regulations 1992 in workplaces where those Regulations apply. The facilities should be conveniently accessible to the working area and to washing facilities, and users should wash before eating or drinking, etc in order to reduce the risk of ingestion.

7

Regulation 8

Use of control measures etc

Regulation

(1) Every employer who provides any control measure, personal protective equipment or other thing or facility pursuant to these Regulations shall take all reasonable steps to ensure that it is properly used or applied as the case may be.

(2) Every employee shall make full and proper use of any control measure, personal protective equipment or other thing or facility provided pursuant to these Regulations and shall take all reasonable steps to ensure it is returned after use to any accommodation provided for it and, if he discovers any defect therein, shall report it forthwith to his employer.

8

General ACOP

50 Procedures should be established by the employer to ensure that control measures, items of personal protective equipment and any other thing or facility are properly used or applied. They should include:

(a) visual checks at appropriate intervals to ensure that control measures are being properly used or applied;

(b) prompt remedial action where necessary.

51 Employees should use the control measures in the way they are intended to be used and should, in particular:

(a) use the control measures provided for materials, plant and processes;

(b) wear in a proper manner the personal protective equipment provided;

(c) store the personal protective equipment when not in use in the accommodation provided;

(d) remove any protective equipment which could cause contamination before eating, drinking or smoking;

(e) practise a high standard of personal hygiene, and make proper use of the facilities provided for washing, showering or bathing and for eating and drinking;

(f) report promptly to management any defects discovered in any control measure, device or facility, or any item of personal protective equipment.

8

Regulation 9

Maintenance, examination and test of control measures etc

Regulation

(1) Every employer who provides any control measure to meet the requirements of regulation 7 shall ensure that it is maintained in an efficient state, in efficient working order and in good repair and, in the case of personal protective equipment, in a clean condition.

(2) Where engineering controls are provided to meet the requirements of regulation 7, the employer shall ensure that thorough examinations and tests of those engineering controls are carried out -

(a) in the case of local exhaust ventilation plant, at least once every 14 months, or for local exhaust ventilation plant used in conjunction with a process specified in Column 1 of Schedule 4, at not more than the interval specified in the corresponding entry in Column 2 of that Schedule;

9

Regulation

(b) in any other case, at suitable intervals.

(3) Where respiratory protective equipment (other than disposable respiratory protective equipment) is provided to meet the requirements of regulation 7, the employer shall ensure that at suitable intervals thorough examinations and, where appropriate, tests of that equipment are carried out.

(4) Every employer shall keep a suitable record of the examinations and tests carried out in pursuance of paragraphs (2) and (3) and of any repairs carried out as a result of those examinations and tests, and that record or a suitable summary thereof shall be kept available for at least 5 years from the date on which it was made.

9

General ACOP

52 The objective of this regulation is to ensure that all control measures which have been provided to meet the requirements of regulation 7(1) and when being used for that purpose perform as originally intended, and thereby continue effectively to prevent or adequately control exposure of employees to substances hazardous to health. Any defect which could result in reduced efficiency or effectiveness and reduced levels of protection should be detected and remedied as soon as possible.

53 The requirement is restricted to control of exposure so that the duty to maintain ceases to apply when people are not exposed to substances hazardous to health (eg during periods when a process is shut down). However, at times where the existing control measures are inoperative, the process should be discontinued, or alternative measures used.

54 Regulation 9(1) gives the definition of 'maintained' and therefore 'maintenance' in the context of this regulation means any work carried out to sustain the efficiency of control measures, not just work carried out by maintenance workers. It includes visual checks, inspection, testing, preventive servicing and remedial work.

Maintenance of all control measures

55 All engineering control measures in use should receive a visual check, where possible and without undue risk to maintenance personnel, at least once every week.

56 Preventive servicing procedures should specify which engineering control measures require servicing, the nature of the servicing that should be carried out to each of them, when the task should be carried out, the allocation of responsibility and how any defects disclosed should be put right.

57 Where the control measures include operational procedures, these should be reviewed periodically to ensure that they are still effective.

58 In accordance with the requirements of regulation 12(3), whoever carries out any function for the purposes of regulation 9 should be competent to do so.

Control measures subject to thorough examination and test

Engineering controls

In all cases

59 Where engineering control measures (eg those mentioned in this General ACOP under regulation 7, paragraph 33(a)-(e)) are provided to control exposure, they must be thoroughly examined and tested at suitable or specified intervals. This is to ensure that these control measures are continuing to

9

perform as originally intended. The results of each thorough examination and test should be compared with the assessment carried out under regulation 6 and the requirements of regulation 7 with regard to control. Any defects disclosed as a result of the examination or test should be remedied as soon as possible or within such time as the examiner directs.

60 The nature and content of the thorough examination and test depend on the particular engineering control under consideration (ie its inherent reliability in sustaining the level of control over the hazardous substance intended for the purposes of regulation 7) and the nature and degree of risk posed by the hazardous substance (ie the consequences of deterioration or failure of the control measure). In the case of local exhaust ventilation (LEV) plant, the requirements set out in paragraph 64 should be met. In all other cases, the examination and test should be sufficient, but no more extensive than is necessary to disclose any defect or any latent defect.

61 The same considerations should be applied in determining suitable intervals between examinations and tests: the frequency should be commensurate with the extent of the risk in the event of failure or deterioration of the control measure. (For LEV plant, see regulation 9(2)(a).) The frequency of examinations may need to be increased with the increasing age of the engineering control concerned. Re-examination and reassessment will also be required in the event of any significant change to the plant or process.

62 All necessary co-operation should be given to the person carrying out the thorough examination and test to enable the examination and test to be carried out correctly and fully.

63 A suitable record of each thorough examination and test should be kept. In the case of LEV plant, the record should contain the particulars listed in paragraph 65. In all other cases, similar information should be kept, modified to be relevant to the type of engineering control concerned.

Local exhaust ventilation (LEV) plant

64 In the case of all LEV plant installed to meet the requirements of regulation 7, whether fixed or portable, including microbiological safety cabinets, the examination and test should be sufficient to provide correct information for the particulars listed in paragraph 65.

65 A suitable record, containing at least the following particulars, should be kept in respect of each thorough examination and test of LEV plant:

(a) name and address of employer responsible for the plant;

(b) identification and location of the LEV plant, process, and hazardous substance concerned;

(c) date of last thorough examination and test;

(d) conditions at time of test: normal production or special conditions (eg maximum use, stood down);

(e) information about the LEV plant which shows:

 (i) its intended operating performance for controlling the hazardous substance for the purposes of regulation 7 - see notes (1) and (2) on page 20;

9

(ii) whether the plant now still achieved the same performance;

(iii) if not, the repairs required to achieve that performance;

(f) methods used to make judgement at (e)(ii) and (e)(iii) (eg visual, pressure measurements, air flow measurements, dust lamp, air sampling, filter integrity tests);

(g) date of examination and test;

(h) name, designation and employer of person carrying out examination and test;

(i) signature or unique authentication of person carrying out examination and test;

(j) details of repairs carried out - see note (3) on this page.

Notes

(1) If there is no information available for item (e)(i), this will indicate a need for the employer to make a further assessment in accordance with regulation 6 to show compliance with regulation 7.

(2) Examples of the details which should be available in respect of the main components of the LEV system are as follows:

Enclosures/hoods - maximum number to be in use at any one time; location or position; static pressure behind each hood or extraction point; face velocity.

Ducting - dimensions; transport velocity; volume flow.

Filter/collector - specification; volume flow; static pressures at inlet, outlet and across filter.

Fan or air mover - specification; volume flow; static pressure at inlet; direction of rotation.

Systems which return exhaust air to the workplace - filter efficiency; concentration of contaminant in returned air.

(3) Details to be completed by employer responsible for the LEV plant. The effectiveness of the repairs should be proved by a re-test.

Respiratory protective equipment (RPE)

66 Thorough examinations and, where appropriate, tests of items of RPE, other than one-shift disposable respirators, should be made at least once every month, and more frequently where the conditions are particularly severe. However, in the case of half-mask respirators used only occasionally, for short spells, against dusts or fumes of relatively low toxicity, longer intervals between examinations may be suitable. In such cases, suitable intervals should be determined by the person responsible for the management of all aspects of the maintenance of RPE, but in any event, the intervals should not exceed three months.

9

67 The examinations should comprise a thorough visual examination of all parts of the respirator or breathing apparatus, in particular of the integrity of

General ACOP

straps, facepieces, filters and valves. In the case of RPE incorporating compressed gas cylinders or electric motors, tests should be made of the condition and efficiency of those parts, including tests of the pressure in the cylinders. In the case of airline-fed RPE, the volume flow and quality of the supplied air should be tested. Any defects disclosed by the examination or test should be remedied before further use.

68 The record of each thorough examination and test carried out should include:

(a) name and address of employer responsible for the RPE;

(b) particulars of the equipment and of the distinguishing number or mark, together with a description sufficient to identify it, and the name of the maker;

(c) date of examination and name and signature or unique authentication of person carrying out examination and test;

(d) condition of the equipment and particulars of any defect found, including in the cases of canister or filter respirators, the state of the canister and of the integrity of the filter;

(e) in the case of compressed oxygen or air apparatus, the pressure of oxygen or air, as the case may be, in the supply cylinder;

(f) in the case of airline-fed apparatus, the volume flow and quality of the supplied air. See also note (1).

Notes

(1) Where the air supply is from mobile compressors, this test should be made immediately prior to the first use in any new location.

(2) In the case of half-mask respirators used occasionally against dusts or fumes of relatively low toxicity, it will be sufficient for the record to be restricted to the particulars at (a), (c) and (d), provided that it can otherwise be readily established to which item of RPE the record relates.

Records

69 Records may be kept in any format. They should be readily available on request for inspection by employees or their representatives, or by inspectors appointed by the relevant enforcing authority or employment medical advisers.

9

Regulation 10

Monitoring exposure at the workplace

Regulation

(1) In any case in which -

(a) it is requisite for ensuring the maintenance of adequate control of the exposure of employees to substances hazardous to health; or

(b) it is otherwise requisite for protecting the health of employees,

the employer shall ensure that the exposure of employees to substances hazardous to health is monitored in accordance with a suitable procedure.

10

Regulation

(2) Where a substance or process is specified in Column 1 of Schedule 5, monitoring shall be carried out at least at the frequency specified in the corresponding entry in Column 2 of that Schedule.

(3) The employer shall keep a suitable record of any monitoring carried out for the purpose of this regulation and that record or a suitable summary thereof shall be kept available -

(a) where the record is representative of the personal exposures of identifiable employees, for at least 40 years;

10

(b) in any other case, for at least 5 years.

General ACOP

70 Where requisite, monitoring for the purpose of regulation 10(1) means the use of valid and suitable occupational hygiene techniques to derive a quantitative estimate of the exposure of employees to substances hazardous to health. In the case of airborne contaminants this measurement will normally involve the collection of a sample from the employee's breathing zone using personal sampling equipment, but may, where appropriate, involve the periodic or continuous sampling of the atmosphere at the workplace. However, if monitoring specified substances or processes listed in Schedule 5 for the purposes of regulation 10(2), it may be sufficient to carry out inspection and testing of the control measures alone, provided the requirements in paragraphs 59-63 have been diligently applied. This should normally be supported by some initial sampling of the atmosphere, and further sampling if appropriate, to provide the baseline data for deriving suitable and adequate settings for the control measures concerned.

71 In accordance with the requirements of regulation 12(3), whoever carries out the monitoring should be competent to do so.

Where requisite

72 Monitoring is requisite when any of the following circumstances apply, unless suitable procedures for monitoring do not exist, or cannot be devised, or it is immediately obvious whether control is adequate:

(a) when failure or deterioration of the control measures could result in a serious health effect, either because of the toxicity of the substance or because of the extent of potential exposure, or both;

(b) when measurement is necessary so as to be sure that a maximum exposure limit or occupational exposure standard or any self-imposed working standard is not exceeded; or

(c) when necessary as an additional check on the effectiveness of any control measure provided in accordance with regulation 7, and always in the case of the substances or processes specified in Schedule 5.

73 Recommendations for monitoring made in any relevant technical literature, including HSE Guidance Notes, indicate some of the situations where monitoring needs to be carried out, if any of the circumstances described in paragraph 72 apply.

Procedures for monitoring

74 Procedures for monitoring should establish when and how it is to be done, the measuring and sampling methods to be used, sites and frequency of sampling and how the results are to be interpreted.

10

General ACOP

75 Where the assessment under regulation 6 shows that monitoring is required, employers should decide how frequently it should be carried out. The frequency will depend on the factors considered by the assessment, including: the processes and substances present in the workplace; the control measures used and how they are tested and maintained; and the closeness of exposure to the occupational exposure limit. Where monitoring is required for continuous processes or regular activities, it should be carried out at least once every 12 months, except for the specific substances and processes listed in Schedule 5 for which more frequent monitoring is required. For infrequent activities that take place at intervals exceeding 12 months, monitoring should be carried out during the activities concerned. Further guidance on routine monitoring can be found in the HSE publication *Monitoring strategies for toxic substances* (see page 15).

76 Where groups of employees are performing identical or similar tasks and are consequently being exposed to similar risks to health, sampling may be carried out on a group basis, provided that it is representative of each individual within the group.

77 Advice on suitable sampling techniques and methods of analysis is contained in guidance provided by the Health and Safety Executive in the Methods for the Determination of Hazardous Substances (MDHS) series and may also be obtained, for instance, from suppliers of substances, or occupational health textbooks.

Records

78 To be regarded as suitable, a record should provide sufficient information to determine:

(a) when the monitoring was done and what the results were;

(b) what monitoring procedures were adopted, including the duration; and

(c) the locations where samples were taken, the operations in progress at the time and, in the case of personal samples, the names of the individuals concerned.

79 The records may be kept in any format but in all cases the information should be readily retrievable and in an easily understood form. It should be kept in such a way that the results can be compared with any health records required under regulation 11.

80 Records of monitoring should be available to employees or their representatives in accordance with regulation 12(2)(a) and to inspectors appointed by the relevant enforcing authority or employment medical advisers.

10

Regulation 11 Health surveillance

Regulation

(1) Where it is appropriate for the protection of the health of his employees who are, or are liable to be, exposed to a substance hazardous to health, the employer shall ensure that such employees are under suitable health surveillance.

(2) Health surveillance shall be treated as being appropriate where -

(a) the employee is exposed to one of the substances specified in Column 1 of Schedule 6 and is engaged in a process specified in Column 2 of that Schedule, unless that exposure is not significant; or

11

Regulation

(b) *the exposure of the employee to a substance hazardous to health is such that an identifiable disease or adverse health effect may be related to the exposure, there is a reasonable likelihood that the disease or effect may occur under the particular conditions of his work and there are valid techniques for detecting indications of the disease or the effect.*

(3) The employer shall ensure that a health record, containing particulars approved by the Executive, in respect of each of his employees to whom paragraph (1) relates is made and maintained and that that record or a copy thereof is kept in a suitable form for at least 40 years from the date of the last entry made in it.

(4) Where an employer who holds records in accordance with paragraph (3) ceases to trade, he shall forthwith notify the Executive thereof in writing and offer those records to the Executive.

(5) If an employee is exposed to a substance specified in Schedule 6 and is engaged in a process specified therein, the health surveillance required under paragraph (1) shall include medical surveillance under the supervision of an employment medical adviser or appointed doctor at intervals of not more than 12 months or at such shorter intervals as the employment medical adviser or appointed doctor may require.

(6) Where an employee is subject to medical surveillance in accordance with paragraph (5) and an employment medical adviser or appointed doctor has certified by an entry in the health record of that employee that in his professional opinion that employee should not be engaged in work which exposes him to that substance or that he should only be so engaged under conditions specified in the record, the employer shall not permit the employee to be engaged in such work except in accordance with the conditions, if any, specified in the health record, unless that entry has been cancelled by an employment medical adviser or appointed doctor.

(7) Where an employee is subject to medical surveillance in accordance with paragraph (5) and an employment medical adviser or appointed doctor has certified by an entry in his health record that medical surveillance should be continued after his exposure to that substance has ceased, the employer shall ensure that the medical surveillance of that employee is continued in accordance with that entry while he is employed by the employer, unless that entry has been cancelled by an employment medical adviser or appointed doctor.

(8) On reasonable notice being given, the employer shall allow any of his employees access to the health record which relates to him.

(9) An employee to whom this regulation applies shall, when required by his employer and at the cost of the employer, present himself during his working hours for such health surveillance procedures as may be required for the purposes of paragraph (1) and, in the case of an employee who is subject to medical surveillance in accordance with paragraph (5), shall furnish the employment medical adviser or appointed doctor with such information concerning his health as the employment medical adviser or appointed doctor may reasonably require.

(10) Where, for the purpose of carrying out his functions under these Regulations, an employment medical adviser or appointed doctor requires to inspect any workplace or any record kept for the purposes of these Regulations, the employer shall permit him to do so.

11 *(11) Where an employee or an employer is aggrieved by a decision recorded in the health record by an employment medical adviser or appointed doctor to suspend an employee from work which exposes him to a substance hazardous to*

Regulation

health (or to impose conditions on such work), he may, by an application in writing to the Executive within 28 days of the date on which he was notified of the decision, apply for that decision to be reviewed in accordance with a procedure approved for the purposes of this paragraph by the Health and Safety Commission, and the result of that review shall be notified to the employee and employer and entered in the health record in accordance with the approved procedure.

(12) In this regulation -

"appointed doctor" means a registered medical practitioner who is appointed for the time being in writing by the Executive for the purposes of this regulation;

"employment medical adviser" means an employment medical adviser appointed under section 56 of the 1974 Act;

"health surveillance" includes biological monitoring.

11

General ACOP

Purpose of health surveillance

81 The objectives of health surveillance, where employees are exposed to substances hazardous to health in the course of their work, are:

(a) the protection of the health of individual employees by the detection at as early a stage as possible of adverse changes which may be attributed to exposure to substances hazardous to health;

(b) to assist in the evaluation of the measures taken to control exposure;

(c) the collection, maintenance and use of data for the detection and evaluation of hazards to health;

(d) to assess, in relation to specific work activities involving biological agents, the immunity of employees.

The results of any health surveillance procedures should lead to some action which will be of benefit to the health of employees. The options and criteria for action should be established before undertaking health surveillance as well as the method of recording, analysis and interpretation of the results of health surveillance.

Suitable health surveillance

82 Health surveillance will always include the keeping of an individual health record (see paragraph 95) and, in addition, it can include a range of procedures, one or more of which is capable of achieving the objectives set out in paragraph 81. The procedure(s) which are most suitable in the particular case should be selected. The range of health surveillance procedures for the purpose of this regulation can be considered to include:

(a) biological monitoring, ie the measurement and assessment of workplace agents or their metabolites either in tissues, secreta, excreta or expired air, or any combination of these in exposed workers;

(b) biological effect monitoring, ie the measurement and assessment of early biological effects in exposed workers;

(c) medical surveillance (ie both surveillance under the supervision of an employment medical adviser or an appointed doctor for the purpose of regulation 11(5) and under the supervision of a registered medical practitioner), which may include clinical examinations and measurements

11

of physiological and psychological effects of exposure to hazardous substances in the workplace as indicated by alterations in body function or constituents;

(d) enquiries about symptoms, inspection or examination by a suitably qualified person (eg an occupational health nurse);

(e) inspection by a responsible person (eg for chrome ulceration by supervisor, manager, etc);

(f) review of records and occupational history during and after exposure; the review should be used to check the correctness of the assessment of risks to health made under regulation 6 and indicate whether the assessment requires review.

These procedures are not mutually exclusive and the results of one might indicate the need for another, eg the results of biological monitoring may show a need for other health surveillance procedures.

83 Where a method of health surveillance is specified for a particular substance in any Approved Code of Practice under these Regulations, that method should preferably be used.

84 Regulation 11(5) specifies the frequency of medical surveillance carried out under the supervision of employment medical advisers or appointed doctors. This is at intervals not exceeding 12 months, or at such shorter intervals as the employment medical adviser or appointed doctor requires. The exact nature of the examination is at the direction and discretion of the employment medical adviser or appointed doctor.

85 Other health surveillance procedures should be carried out either under the supervision of a registered medical practitioner or, where appropriate, by a suitably qualified person (eg an occupational health nurse) or a responsible person. A responsible person is someone appointed by the employer who is competent, in accordance with regulation 12(3), to carry out the relevant procedure and who is charged with reporting to the employer the conclusions of the procedure.

Where health surveillance is appropriate

86 Health surveillance, which must include medical surveillance under the supervision of an employment medical adviser or appointed doctor, is appropriate for workers liable to be exposed to the substances and engaged in the processes listed in Schedule 6 to the Regulations.

87 Health surveillance, including the keeping of health records, will also be appropriate for workers exposed to any other substance which fulfils the criteria listed in regulation 11(2)(b). Any judgement as to the likelihood that a disease or adverse health effect may occur must be related to the nature and degree of exposure. The judgement should include assessment of available epidemiology, information on human exposure, and human and animal toxicological data, as well as extrapolation from information about analogous substances or situations.

88 Valid techniques are those of acceptably high sensitivity and specificity which can detect abnormalities related to the nature and degree of exposure. The criteria for interpreting the data should be known (eg this may require the establishment of normal values and action levels). The aim should be to establish health surveillance procedures which are safe, easy to perform, non-invasive and acceptable to employees.

11

Substance/process		*Typical procedure*
(a)	Substances of recognised systemic toxicity.	Appropriate clinical or laboratory investigations.
(b)	Substances known to cause occupational asthma.	Enquiries seeking evidence of respiratory symptoms related to work.
(c)	Substances known to cause severe dermatitis.	Skin inspection by a responsible person.
(d)	(i) Electrolytic plating or oxidation of metal articles by use of an electrolyte containing chromic acid or other chromium compounds; (ii) Contact with chrome solutions in dyeing processes using dichromate of potassium or sodium; (iii) Contact with chrome solutions in processes of liming and tanning of raw hides and skins (including re-tanning of tanned hides or skins).	Skin inspection by a responsible person.

89 In the particular conditions of work, should any of the criteria in paragraphs 87 and 88 not apply, health surveillance procedures should be reviewed and subsequently modified or discontinued as appropriate.

90 Categories where health surveillance is appropriate under the criteria in regulation 11(2)(b) are given in the table above together with information on typical forms of surveillance. Other examples are given in relevant technical literature including HSE Guidance Notes. In all these cases surveillance should be carried out, unless there is no significant risk to health. The list is not definitive and there will be other instances where the criteria in regulation 11(2)(b) indicate that health surveillance is required.

91 The collection, maintenance and review of health records (see Appendix paragraph l(a)) may protect the health of workers through the detection and evaluation of risks to health. In some cases, the only health surveillance required is the collection and maintenance of those records - examples are:

(a) known or suspected carcinogens (eg substances defined as carcinogens in regulation 2(1)) other than those already included in Schedule 6 to the Regulations or in paragraph 90;

(b) machine-made mineral fibres, also known as man-made mineral fibres and MMMF;

(c) rubber manufacturing and processing giving rise to rubber process dust and rubber fume (other than the relevant entry in Column 2, Schedule 6);

(d) leather dust in boot and shoe manufacture, arising during preparation and finishing.

Significant exposure

11

92 If, following a suitable and sufficient assessment, it can be shown under the circumstances of exposure to a substance hazardous to health, that such

General ACOP

exposure is most unlikely to result in any disease or adverse health effect, then exposure can be deemed not to be significant. Further information about significant exposure can be found in other Approved Codes of Practice under these Regulations and in relevant technical literature, including HSE Guidance Notes.

Continuing health surveillance after cessation of exposure

93 In certain circumstances it may be appropriate for an employer to continue health surveillance of his employees (while they remain his employees) after exposure to a substance hazardous to health has ceased. Cases where this will be of benefit to workers may be those where an adverse effect on health may be anticipated after a latent period and where it is believed that the effect can be reliably detected at a sufficiently early stage. Examples of substances which normally entail continuing health surveillance after cessation of exposure are those which cause cancer of the urinary tract.

Facilities for health surveillance

94 Where health surveillance procedures are carried out at the employer's premises, suitable facilities should be available. In cases where examinations and inspections are required, facilities should include a room which is clean, warm, well-ventilated, suitably furnished and having a washbasin, equipped with hot and cold running water, soap and a clean towel. (If it is not reasonably practicable to provide hot and cold running water, means of heating water should be provided in the room.) The room should be set aside for the exclusive purpose of health surveillance when required and provision should be made for privacy. Where the number of employees to be examined or assessed is substantial, a suitable waiting area should be provided. An adjacent WC with hand-washing facilities should be available for employees when providing specimens for biological monitoring or biological effect monitoring.

Health record

95 A health record, to be kept in all cases where health surveillance is required by the Regulations, should contain at least the information set out in the Appendix to this General ACOP. These particulars are approved by the Health and Safety Executive.

In a suitable form

96 In addition to keeping the particulars given in the Appendix, an index or list of the names of people undergoing, or who have undergone, health surveillance should be kept. The record should be kept in a form compatible with and capable of being linked to those required by regulation 10 for monitoring of exposure, so that, where appropriate, the nature and degree of exposure can be compared with effects on health.

11

Regulation 12

Information, instruction and training for persons who may be exposed to substances hazardous to health

Regulation

12

(1) An employer who undertakes work which may expose any of his employees to substances hazardous to health shall provide that employee with such information, instruction and training as is suitable and sufficient for him to know -

(a) the risks to health created by such exposure; and

Regulation

(b) *the precautions which should be taken.*

(2) Without prejudice to the generality of paragraph (1), the information provided under that paragraph shall include -

(a) *information on the results of any monitoring of exposure at the workplace in accordance with regulation 10 and, in particular, in the case of any substance hazardous to health for which a maximum exposure limit has been approved, the employee or his representatives shall be informed forthwith, if the results of such monitoring show that the maximum exposure limit has been exceeded; and*

(b) *information on the collective results of any health surveillance undertaken in accordance with regulation 11 in a form calculated to prevent it from being identified as relating to any particular person.*

(3) Every employer shall ensure that any person (whether or not his employee) who carries out any work in connection with the employer's duties under these Regulations has the necessary information, instruction and training.

12

General ACOP

97 The information provided to employees and other people on the premises in accordance with regulation 12 should include, in particular:

(a) the nature and degree of the risks to health arising as a consequence of exposure, including any factors that may influence that risk, such as the substance involved and factors that may increase the risk, eg smoking;

(b) the control measures adopted, the reasons for these, and how to use them properly;

(c) the reasons for personal protective equipment and clothing, and the jobs where these are necessary;

(d) monitoring procedures, including arrangements for access to results and notification if a maximum exposure limit is exceeded;

(e) the role of health surveillance, their duty to attend for health surveillance procedures, and arrangements for access to individual health records (see regulation 11(8)) and the collective results of health surveillance.

98 This information should also be made available to employees or their representatives in accordance with the Safety Representatives and Safety Committees Regulations 1977 and the Health and Safety (Consultation with Employees) Regulations 1996.

Instruction

99 Instruction must be such as to ensure that people at work on the premises do not endanger themselves or others through exposure to substances hazardous to health. In particular, the instruction must be sufficient and suitable for them to:

(a) know what they should do, what precautions they should take and when they should take them;

(b) know what cleaning, storage and disposal procedures are required, why they are required and when they are to be carried out;

(c) know the procedures to be followed in an emergency.

12

General ACOP

Training

100 Training must be such as to ensure that people at work on the premises can effectively apply and use:

(a) the methods of control;

(b) the personal protective equipment;

(c) the emergency measures.

People carrying out work on behalf of employer

101 As required by regulation 12(3), any person who carries out any work on behalf of the employer in relation to any of his duties under the Regulations should possess sufficient knowledge, skill and experience to be able to perform that work effectively. The employer should therefore ensure that the person to whom any work is delegated is competent for that purpose and this may entail engaging expertise from outside the undertaking. When this occurs, the employer will still need to ensure that the people engaged receive sufficient information about the particular circumstances of the work. Some tasks under the Regulations may require a range of expertise that may not be possessed by a single person; under the Interpretation Act 1978 'person' includes a body of persons corporate or unincorporate.

12

Regulation 13

Provisions relating to certain fumigations

Regulation

(1) This regulation shall apply to fumigations in which the fumigant used or intended to be used is hydrogen cyanide, phosphine or methyl bromide, except that paragraph (2) shall not apply to fumigations using the fumigant specified in Column 1 of Schedule 7 when the nature of the fumigation is that specified in the corresponding entry in Column 2 of that Schedule.

(2) An employer shall not undertake any fumigation to which this regulation applies unless he has -

(a) notified the persons specified in Part I of Schedule 8 of his intention to undertake the fumigation; and

(b) provided to those persons the information specified in Part II of that Schedule,

at least 24 hours in advance, or such shorter time in advance, as the persons required to be notified may agree.

(3) An employer who undertakes a fumigation to which this regulation applies shall ensure that, before the fumigant is released, suitable warning notices have been affixed at all points of reasonable access to the premises or to those parts of the premises in which the fumigation is to be carried out and that after the fumigation has been completed, and the premises are safe to enter, those warning notices are removed.

13

General ACOP

102 Schedule 7 to the Regulations lists a number of fumigations exempted from the notification requirements of regulation 13. For all three specified gases, these exemptions include fumigations carried out for research and also fumigations in fumigation chambers.

13

Regulation 14

Exemption certificates

Regulation

14

(1) Subject to paragraph (2) the Executive may, by a certificate in writing, exempt any person or class of persons or any substance or class of substances from all or any of the requirements or prohibitions imposed by these Regulations and any such exemption may be granted subject to conditions and to a limit of time and may be revoked by a certificate in writing at any time.

(2) The Executive shall not grant any such exemption unless having regard to the circumstances of the case and, in particular, to -

(a) the conditions, if any, which it proposes to attach to the exemption; and

(b) any other requirements imposed by or under any enactments which apply to the case,

it is satisfied that the health and safety of persons who are likely to be affected by the exemption will not be prejudiced in consequence of it.

Regulation 15

Extension outside Great Britain

Regulation

15

(1) Subject to paragraph (2), these Regulations shall apply to and in relation to any activity outside Great Britain to which sections 1 to 59 and 80 to 82 of the 1974 Act apply by virtue of article 4, 6 or 8 of the Health and Safety at Work etc. Act 1974 (Application outside Great Britain) Order 1995[(a)] as those provisions apply within Great Britain.

(2) These Regulations shall not extend to Northern Ireland except insofar as they relate to imports of substances and articles referred to in regulation 4(2) into the United Kingdom.

(a) SI 1995/263.

Regulation 16

Defence in proceedings for contravention of these Regulations

Regulation

16

In any proceedings for an offence consisting of a contravention of these Regulations it shall be a defence for any person to prove that he took all reasonable precautions and exercised all due diligence to avoid the commission of that offence.

Regulation 17

Exemptions relating to the Ministry of Defence etc

Regulation

17

(1) In this regulation, any reference to -

(a) "visiting forces" is a reference to visiting forces within the meaning of any provision of Part I of the Visiting Forces Act 1952[(a)]; and

(b) "headquarters or organisation" is a reference to a headquarters or organisation designated for the purposes of the International Headquarters and Defence Organisations Act 1964[(b)].

(a) 1952 c.67.
(b) 1964 c.5.

Regulation

(2) The Secretary of State for Defence may, in the interests of national security, by a certificate in writing exempt -

(a) Her Majesty's Forces;

(b) visiting forces;

(c) any member of a visiting force working in or attached to any headquarters or organisation; or

(d) any person engaged in work involving substances hazardous to health, if that person is under the direct supervision of a representative of the Secretary of State for Defence,

from all or any of the requirements or prohibitions imposed by these Regulations and any such exemption may be granted subject to conditions and to a limit of time and may be revoked at any time by a certificate in writing, except that, where any such exemption is granted, suitable arrangements shall be made for the assessment of the health risks created by the work involving substances hazardous to health and for adequately controlling the exposure to those substances of persons to whom the exemption relates.

(3) Regulation 11(11) shall not apply in relation to -

(a) visiting forces; or

(b) any member of a visiting force working in or attached to any headquarters or organisation.

17

General ACOP

103 The power to exempt is available to the Secretary of State for Defence only in times of tension, that is, when the state is under threat or otherwise facing an emergency. Exemptions, if needed, must be in writing and would be issued, after consultation with the Health and Safety Executive, for specific activities and for a limited period only. When an exemption is granted, suitable arrangements should still be made to assess the risk to health from the work and for adequately controlling exposure.

104 A person under the direct supervision of a representative of the Secretary of State for Defence is an employee of the Ministry of Defence, a member of Her Majesty's Forces, or certain people employed on Ministry of Defence premises, for example on a labour-only contract. In the latter case, whether or not there is direct supervision will depend on the nature of the contract. People employed on the premises of defence contractors are most unlikely to be under such direct supervision; for example, Ministry of Defence liaison staff at a defence contractor's premises do not normally exercise direct supervision, and similarly, staff on contracts at universities are not under direct supervision.

17

Regulation 18

Revocations, amendments and savings

Regulation

(1) The following Regulations are revoked -

(a) the Control of Substances Hazardous to Health Regulations 1994[(a)];

(b) the Control of Substances Hazardous to Health (Amendment) Regulations 1996[(b)];

18

(a) SI 1994/3246.
(b) SI 1996/3138.

Regulation

18

(c) the Control of Substances Hazardous to Health (Amendment) Regulations 1997[a]*;*

(d) the Control of Substances Hazardous to Health (Amendment) Regulations 1998[b]*.*

(2) In the definition of "biological agent" in regulation 2(1) of the Reporting of Injuries, Diseases and Dangerous Occurrences Regulations 1995[c]*, for the number "1994" substitute "1999".*

(3) In the Health and Safety (Fees) Regulations 1997[d] *-*

(a) in regulation 3(1)(e), for the number "1994" substitute "1999";

(b) in column 1 of entry (c) in the Table in Schedule 6, for the number "1994" substitute "1999"; and

(c) in column 2 of entry (c) in the Table in Schedule 6, for the reference "S.I. 1994/3246" substitute "S.I. 1999/437".

(4) Any record or register required to be kept under any regulations revoked by paragraph (1) shall, notwithstanding those revocations, be kept in the same manner and for the same period as specified in those regulations as if these Regulations had not been made, except that the Executive may approve the keeping of records at a place or in a form other than at the place where, or in the form in which, records were required to be kept under the regulations so revoked.

(a) SI 1997/11.
(b) SI 1998/1357.
(c) SI 1995/3163.
(d) SI 1997/2505.

Regulation 19

Extension of meaning of "work"

Regulation

19

For the purposes of Part I of the 1974 Act the meaning of "work" shall be extended to include any activity involving the consignment, storage or use of any of the biological agents listed in Part V of Schedule 3 and the meaning of "at work" shall be extended accordingly, and in that connection the references to employer in paragraphs 12 and 13 of that Schedule include references to any person carrying on such an activity.

Regulation 20

Modification of section 3(2) of the 1974 Act

Regulation

20

Section 3(2) of the 1974 Act shall be modified in relation to an activity involving the consignment, storage or use of any of the biological agents referred to in regulation 19 so as to have effect as if the reference therein to a self-employed person is a reference to any person who is not an employer or an employee and the reference therein to his undertaking includes a reference to such an activity.

Schedule 1

Other substances and processes to which the definition of "carcinogen" relates

Regulation 2(1)

Schedule

1

Aflatoxins

Arsenic

Auramine manufacture

Calcining, sintering or smelting of nickel copper matte or acid leaching or electrorefining of roasted matte

Coal soots, coal tar, pitch and coal tar fumes

Hardwood dusts

Isopropyl alcohol manufacture (strong acid process)

Leather dust in boot and shoe manufacture, arising during preparation and finishing

Magenta manufacture

Mustard gas (β, β'-dichlorodiethyl sulphide)

Rubber manufacturing and processing giving rise to rubber process dust and rubber fume

Used engine oils

Schedule 2

Prohibition of certain substances hazardous to health for certain purposes

Regulation 4(1)

Schedule

	Column 1 *Description of substance*	*Column 2* *Purpose for which the substance is prohibited*
1	2-naphthylamine; benzidine; 4-aminodiphenyl; 4-nitrodiphenyl; their salts and any substance containing any of those compounds, in a total concentration equal to or greater than 0.1 per cent by mass.	Manufacture and use for all purposes including any manufacturing process in which a substance described in Column 1 of this item is formed.
2	Sand or other substance containing free silica.	Use as an abrasive for blasting articles in any blasting apparatus.
3	A substance - (a) containing compounds of silicon calculated as silica to the extent of more than 3 per cent by weight of dry material, other than natural sand, zirconium silicate (zircon), calcined china clay, calcined aluminous fireclay, sillimanite, calcined or fused alumina, olivine; or (b) composed of or containing dust or other matter deposited from a fettling or blasting process.	Use as a parting material in connection with the making of metal castings.
4	Carbon disulphide.	Use in the cold-cure process of vulcanising in the proofing of cloth with rubber.
5	Oils other than white oil, or oil of entirely animal or vegetable origin or entirely of mixed animal and vegetable origin.	Use for oiling the spindles of self-acting mules.
6	Ground or powdered flint or quartz other than natural sand.	Use in relation to the manufacture or decoration of pottery for the following purposes: (a) the placing of ware for the biscuit fire; (b) the polishing of ware; (c) as the ingredient of a wash for saggars, trucks, bats, cranks, or other articles used in supporting ware during firing; and (d) as dusting or supporting powder in potters' shops.
7	Ground or powdered flint or quartz other than - (a) natural sand; or (b) ground or powdered flint or quartz which forms parts of a slop or paste.	Use in relation to the manufacture or decoration of pottery for any purpose except - (a) use in a separate room or building for - (i) the manufacture of powdered flint or quartz, or (ii) the making of frits or glazes or the making of colours or coloured slips for the decoration of pottery; (b) use for the incorporation of the substance into the body of ware in an enclosure in which no person is employed and which is constructed and ventilated to prevent the escape of dust.

2

	Column 1 *Description of substance*	*Column 2* *Purpose for which the substance is prohibited*
8	Dust or powder of a refractory material containing not less than 80 per cent of silica other than natural sand.	Use for sprinkling the moulds of silica bricks, namely bricks or other articles composed of refractory material and containing not less than 80 per cent of silica.
9	White phosphorus.	Use in the manufacture of matches.
10	Hydrogen cyanide.	Use in fumigation except when - (a) released from an inert material in which hydrogen cyanide is absorbed; (b) generated from a gassing powder; or (c) applied from a cylinder through suitable piping and applicators other than for fumigation in the open air to control or kill mammal pests.
11	Benzene and any substance containing benzene in a concentration equal to or greater than 0.1 per cent by mass, other than - (a) motor fuels covered by Council Directive 85/210/EEC (OJ No. L96, 3.4.85, p.25); (b) waste covered by Council Directives 75/442/EEC (OJ No. L194, 25.7.75, p.39), as amended by Council Directive 91/156/EEC (OJ No. L78, 26.3.91, p.32), and 91/689/EEC (OJ No. L377, 31.12.91, p.20).	Use for all purposes except - (a) use in industrial processes; and (b) for the purposes of research and development or for the purpose of analysis.
12	The following substances - Chloroform CAS No. 67-66-3; Carbon Tetrachloride CAS No. 56-23-5; 1,1,2 Trichloroethane CAS No. 79-00-5; 1,1,2,2 Tetrachloroethane CAS No. 79-34-5; 1,1,1,2 Tetrachloroethane CAS No. 630-20-6; Pentachloroethane CAS No. 76-01-7; Vinylidene chloride (1,1 Dichloroethylene) CAS No. 75-35-4; 1,1,1 Trichloroethane CAS No. 71-55-6, and any substance containing one or more of those substances in a concentration equal to or greater than 0.1 per cent by mass, other than - (a) medicinal products; (b) cosmetic products.	Supply for use at work in diffusive applications such as in surface cleaning and the cleaning of fabrics except for the purposes of research and development or for the purpose of analysis.

In this Schedule -

"aerosol dispenser" means an article which consists of a non-reusable receptacle containing a gas compressed, liquefied or dissolved under pressure, with or without liquid, paste or powder and fitted with a release device allowing the contents to be ejected as solid or liquid particles in suspension in a gas, as a foam, paste or powder or in a liquid state;

"blasting apparatus" means apparatus for cleaning, smoothing, roughening or removing of part of the surface of any article by the use as an abrasive of a jet of sand, metal shot or grit or other material propelled by a blast of compressed air or steam or by a wheel;

"CAS No." is the number assigned to a substance by the Chemical Abstract Service;

"cosmetic product" has the meaning assigned to it in regulation 2(1) of the Cosmetic Products (Safety) Regulations 1996[a] (including any aerosol dispenser containing a cosmetic product);

"gassing powder" means a chemical compound in powder form which reacts with atmospheric moisture to generate hydrogen cyanide;

"medicinal product" means a substance or preparation which is -

(a) intended for use as a medicinal product within the meaning of section 130 of the Medicines Act 1968[b]; or

(b) a substance or preparation specified in an order made under section 104 or 105 of the Medicines Act 1968 which is for the time being in force and which directs that specified provisions of that Act shall have effect in relation to that substance or preparation as such provisions have effect in relation to medicinal products within the meaning of that Act;

"use as a parting material" means the application of the material to the surface or parts of the surface of a pattern or of a mould so as to facilitate the separation of the pattern from the mould or the separation of parts of the mould;

"white oil" means a refined mineral oil conforming to a specification approved by the Executive and certified by its manufacturer as so conforming.

(a) SI 1996/2925.
(b) 1968, c.67.

Special provisions relating to biological agents

Regulation 7(10)

Part I Provisions of general application to biological agents

Interpretation

1 In this Schedule -

"cell culture" means the *in-vitro* growth of cells derived from multicellular organisms;

"diagnostic service" means any activity undertaken solely with the intention of -

(a) testing for the presence of or identifying a biological agent,

(b) isolating or identifying other organisms from specimens or samples containing or suspected of containing a biological agent,

(c) analysing specimens or samples from a human patient or animal in which a biological agent is or is suspected of being present for purposes relating to the assessment of the clinical progress, or assistance in the clinical management, of that patient or animal,

and "diagnosis" shall be construed accordingly;

"Group" means one of the four hazard Groups specified in paragraph 3 to which biological agents are assigned.

Application

2 (1) This Schedule shall have effect with a view to protecting employees against risks to their health, whether immediate or delayed, arising from exposure to biological agents except that paragraph 11 shall not apply in relation to a particular biological agent where the results of the assessment made under regulation 6 indicate that -

(a) the activity does not involve a deliberate intention to work with or use that biological agent; and

(b) there is no significant risk to the health of employees associated with that biological agent.

(2) Unless otherwise expressly provided, the provisions of this Schedule shall have effect in addition to and not in substitution for other provisions of these Regulations.

Classification of biological agents

3 (1) The Health and Safety Commission shall approve and publish for the purposes of this Schedule a document, which may be revised or reissued from time to time, entitled *Categorisation of biological agents according to hazard and categories of containment* containing a list of biological agents together with the classification of each agent which it has approved, and any reference in this Schedule to "approved classification" in relation to a particular biological agent

shall be construed as a reference to the classification of that agent which appears in the said document.

(2) Where a biological agent has an approved classification, any reference in these Regulations to a particular Group in relation to that agent shall be taken as a reference to the Group to which that agent has been assigned in that approved classification.

(3) Where a biological agent does not have an approved classification, the employer shall provisionally classify that agent in accordance with sub-paragraph (4) below, having regard to the nature of the agent and the properties of which he may reasonably be expected to be aware.

(4) When provisionally classifying a biological agent the employer shall assign that agent to one of the following Groups according to its level of risk of infection and, if in doubt as to which of two alternative Groups is the most appropriate, he shall assign it to the higher of the two -

(a) Group 1 - unlikely to cause human disease;

(b) Group 2 - can cause human disease and may be a hazard to employees; it is unlikely to spread to the community and there is usually effective prophylaxis or treatment available;

(c) Group 3 - can cause severe human disease and may be a serious hazard to employees; it may spread to the community, but there is usually effective prophylaxis or treatment available;

(d) Group 4 - causes severe human disease and is a serious hazard to employees; it is likely to spread to the community and there is usually no effective prophylaxis or treatment available.

Assessment of health risks

4 Without prejudice to the generality of regulation 6, every employer who intends to carry on any work which is liable to expose his employees to any biological agent shall take account of the Group into which that agent is classified when making an assessment of the risks created by that work.

Prevention of exposure to a biological agent

5 Without prejudice to the generality of regulation 7(1), if the nature of the activity so permits, every employer shall ensure that the exposure of his employees to a particular biological agent is prevented by substituting a biological agent which is less hazardous.

Control of exposure to biological agents

6 (1) Where there is a risk of exposure to a biological agent and it is not otherwise reasonably practicable to prevent that exposure then it shall be adequately controlled, in particular by the following measures which are to be applied in the light of the results of the assessment -

(a) keeping as low as practicable the number of employees exposed or likely to be exposed to the biological agent;

(b) designing work processes and engineering control measures so as to prevent or minimise the release of biological agents into the place of work;

(c) displaying the biohazard sign shown in Part IV of this Schedule and other relevant warning signs;

(d) drawing up plans to deal with accidents involving biological agents;

(e) specifying appropriate decontamination and disinfection procedures;

(f) instituting means for the safe collection, storage and disposal of contaminated waste, including the use of secure and identifiable containers, after suitable treatment where appropriate;

(g) making arrangements for the safe handling and transport of biological agents, or materials that may contain such agents, within the workplace;

(h) specifying procedures for taking, handling and processing samples that may contain biological agents;

(i) providing collective protection measures and, where exposure cannot be adequately controlled by other means, individual protection measures including, in particular, the supply of appropriate protective clothing or other special clothing;

(j) where appropriate, making available effective vaccines for those employees who are not already immune to the biological agent to which they are exposed or are liable to be exposed;

(k) instituting hygiene measures compatible with the aim of preventing or reducing the accidental transfer or release of a biological agent from the workplace, including, in particular -

  (i) the provision of appropriate and adequate washing and toilet facilities, and

  (ii) the prohibition of eating, drinking, smoking and application of cosmetics in working areas where there is a risk of contamination by biological agents.

(2) In this paragraph, "appropriate" in relation to clothing and hygiene measures means appropriate for the risks involved and the conditions at the place where exposure to the risk may occur.

Special control measures for health and veterinary care facilities

7 In health and veterinary care isolation facilities where there are human patients or animals which are, or are suspected of being, infected with a Group 3 or Group 4 biological agent, the employer shall select the most suitable containment measures from those listed in Part II of this Schedule with a view to controlling adequately the risk of infection.

Special control measures for laboratories, animal rooms and industrial processes

8 (1) Every employer who is engaged in any of the activities specified in sub-paragraph (3) below shall ensure that measures taken to control adequately the exposure of his employees to biological agents include, in particular, the most suitable combination of containment measures from those listed in Parts II and III of this Schedule as appropriate, taking into account -

(a) the nature of the activity specified in sub-paragraph (3) below;

(b) the minimum containment level specified in sub-paragraph (4) below;

(c) the assessment of risk made under regulation 6; and

(d) the nature of the biological agent concerned.

(2) An employer who is engaged in -

(a) any of the activities specified in paragraphs (a) and (b) of sub-paragraph (3) below shall select measures from Part II of this Schedule;

(b) the activity specified in paragraph (c) of sub-paragraph (3) below shall select measures from Part III of this Schedule and, subject to sub-paragraph (4) below, when making that selection he may combine measures from different categories of containment on the basis of a risk assessment related to any particular process or part of a process.

(3) The activities referred to in sub-paragraph (1) above are -

(a) research, development, teaching or diagnostic work in laboratories which involves the handling of a Group 2, Group 3 or Group 4 biological agent or material containing such an agent;

(b) keeping or handling of laboratory animals which have been deliberately infected with a Group 2, Group 3 or Group 4 biological agent or which are, or are suspected of being, naturally infected with such an agent; and

(c) industrial processes which involve the use of a Group 2, Group 3 or Group 4 biological agent.

(4) The minimum containment level referred to in sub-paragraph (1) above shall be -

(a) level 2 for activities involving the handling of a Group 2 biological agent;

(b) level 3 for activities involving the handling of a Group 3 biological agent;

(c) level 4 for activities involving the handling of a Group 4 biological agent;

(d) level 2 for laboratories which do not intentionally work with biological agents but handle materials in respect of which there exist uncertainties about the presence of a Group 2, Group 3 or Group 4 biological agent;

(e) level 3 or 4, where appropriate, for laboratories which do not intentionally work with biological agents but where the employer knows or suspects that such a containment level is necessary; except where guidelines approved by the Health and Safety Commission indicate that, in the particular case, a lower containment level is appropriate; and

(f) level 3 for activities where it has not been possible to carry out a conclusive assessment but concerning which it appears that the activity might involve a serious health risk for employees.

Examination and maintenance of personal protective equipment

9 (1) Every employer who provides personal protective equipment, including protective clothing, to meet the requirements of these Regulations as they apply to biological agents shall ensure that it is -

(a) properly stored in a well-defined place;

(b) checked and cleaned at suitable intervals; and

(c) when discovered to be defective, repaired or replaced before further use.

(2) Personal protective equipment which may be contaminated by biological agents shall be -

(a) removed on leaving the working area; and

(b) kept apart from uncontaminated clothing and equipment.

(3) The employer shall ensure that the equipment referred to in sub-paragraph (2) above is subsequently decontaminated and cleaned or, if necessary, destroyed.

Information for employees

10 (1) Every employer shall provide written instructions at the workplace and, if appropriate, display notices which shall include the procedure to be followed in the case of -

(a) an accident or incident which has or may have resulted in the release of a biological agent which could cause severe human disease;

(b) the handling of a Group 4 biological agent or material that may contain such an agent.

(2) Every employee shall report forthwith, to his employer or to any other employee of that employer with specific responsibility for the health and safety of his fellow employees, any accident or incident which has or may have resulted in the release of a biological agent which could cause severe human disease.

(3) Every employer shall inform his employees or their representatives -

(a) forthwith, of any incident which has or may have resulted in the release of a biological agent which could cause severe human disease; and

(b) as soon as practicable thereafter, of -

(i) the causes of such an accident or incident, and

(ii) the measures taken or to be taken to rectify the situation.

List of employees exposed to certain biological agents

11 (1) Subject to paragraph 2(1), every employer shall keep a list of employees exposed to a Group 3 or Group 4 biological agent, indicating the type of work done and, where known, the biological agent to which they have been exposed, and records of exposures, accidents and incidents, as appropriate.

(2) Subject to sub-paragraph (3) below, the list shall be kept for at least 10 years following the last known exposure of the employee concerned.

(3) In the case of those exposures which may result in infections -

(a) with biological agents known to be capable of establishing persistent or latent infections;

(b) that, in the light of present knowledge, are undiagnosable until illness develops many years later;

(c) that have particularly long incubation periods before illness develops;

(d) that result in illnesses which recrudesce at times over a long period despite treatment; or

(e) that may have serious long-term sequelae,

the list shall be kept for 40 years following the last known exposure.

(4) The employment medical adviser or appointed doctor referred to in regulation 11, and any employee of that employer with specific responsibility for the health and safety of his fellow employees, shall have access to the list.

(5) Each employee shall have access to the information on the list which relates to him personally.

Notification of the use of biological agents

12 (1) Subject to sub-paragraphs (5) and (6) below, an employer shall not store or use for the first time one or more biological agents in Group 2, 3 or 4 at particular premises unless he has notified the Executive in writing of his intention to do so at least 30 days in advance or before such shorter time as the Executive may approve and with that notification has furnished the particulars specified in sub-paragraph (3) below.

(2) Subject to sub-paragraphs (5) and (7) below, notification in accordance with sub-paragraph (1) above shall also be made of the storage or use for the first time of -

(a) each subsequent biological agent where that agent is specified in Part V of this Schedule;

(b) each subsequent Group 3 biological agent where that agent does not have an approved classification.

(3) The particulars to be included in the notification referred to in sub-paragraphs (1) and (2) above shall be -

(a) the name and address of the employer and the address of the premises where the biological agent will be stored or used;

(b) the name, qualifications and relevant experience of any employee of that employer with specific responsibility for the health and safety of his fellow employees;

(c) the results of the assessment made under regulation 6;

(d) the Group to which the biological agent has been assigned and, if the agent is specified in Part V of this Schedule or is a Group 3 agent which does not have an approved classification, the identity of the agent; and

(e) the preventive and protective measures that are to be taken.

(4) Where there are substantial changes to processes or procedures of importance to health or safety at work which render the original notification invalid the employer shall notify the Executive forthwith in writing of those changes.

(5) Sub-paragraphs (1) and (2) above shall not apply in relation to a particular biological agent where an intention to store or use that biological agent has been previously notified to the Executive in accordance with the Genetically Modified Organisms (Contained Use) Regulations 1992[a].

(6) Sub-paragraph (1) above shall not apply to an employer who intends to provide a diagnostic service in relation to Group 2 or Group 3 biological agents, other than those Group 3 agents specified in Part V of this Schedule, unless it will involve a process likely to propagate or concentrate that agent.

(7) Sub-paragraph (1) above shall not apply to an employer who intends to provide a diagnostic service unless it will involve a process likely to propagate or concentrate a biological agent which does not have an approved classification.

Notification of the consignment of biological agents

13 (1) An employer shall not consign any of the biological agents specified in Part V of this Schedule or anything containing, or suspected of containing, such an agent to any other premises, whether or not those premises are under his ownership or control, unless he has notified the Executive in writing of his intention to do so at least 30 days in advance or before such shorter time as the Executive may approve and with that notification has furnished the particulars specified in sub-paragraph (4) below.

(2) Sub-paragraph (1) above shall not apply where -

(a) the biological agent or material containing or suspected of containing such an agent is being consigned solely for the purpose of diagnosis;

(b) material containing or suspected of containing the biological agent is being consigned solely for the purpose of disposal; or

(c) the biological agent is or is suspected of being present in a human patient or animal which is being transported for the purpose of medical treatment.

(3) Where a biological agent specified in Part V of this Schedule is imported into Great Britain, the consignee shall give the notice required by sub-paragraph (1) above.

(4) The particulars to be included in the notification referred to in sub-paragraph (1) above shall be -

(a) the identity of the biological agent and the volume of the consignment;

(b) the name of the consignor;

(c) the address of the premises from which it will be transported;

(d) the name of the consignee;

(a) SI 1992/3217, as amended by SI 1996/967, 1998/1548.

(e) the address of the premises to which it shall be transported;

(f) the name of the transport operator responsible for the transportation;

(g) the name of any individual who will accompany the consignment;

(h) the method of transportation;

(i) the packaging and any containment precautions which will be taken;

(j) the route which will be taken; and

(k) the proposed date of transportation.

Notification to the Health Ministers

14 (1) Upon receipt of any notification submitted in accordance with paragraphs 12 or 13 concerning a biological agent specified in Part V of this Schedule, the Executive shall notify the appropriate Health Minister forthwith in writing that that agent is to be or is no longer to be stored, used or consigned.

(2) In sub-paragraph (1) above "Health Minister" means, in respect of England, Scotland or Wales, the Secretary of State concerned with health in that country.

Schedule

Part II Containment measures for health and veterinary care facilities, laboratories and animal rooms

Containment measures	*Containment levels* 2	3	4
1 The workplace is to be separated from any other activities in the same building.	No	Yes	Yes
2 Input air and extract air to the workplace are to be filtered using HEPA or equivalent.	No	Yes, on extract air	Yes, on input and double on extract air
3 Access is to be restricted to authorised persons only.	Yes	Yes	Yes, via air-lock key procedure
4 The workplace is to be sealable to permit disinfection.	No	Yes	Yes
5 Specified disinfection procedures.	Yes	Yes	Yes
6 The workplace is to be maintained at an air pressure negative to atmosphere.	No, unless mechanically ventilated	Yes	Yes
7 Efficient vector control, eg rodents and insects.	Yes, for animal containment	Yes, for animal containment	Yes
8 Surfaces impervious to water and easy to clean.	Yes, for bench	Yes, for bench and floor (and walls for animal containment)	Yes, for bench, floor, walls and ceiling
9 Surfaces resistant to acids, alkalis, solvents, disinfectants.	Yes, for bench	Yes, for bench and floor (and walls for animal containment)	Yes, for bench, floor, walls and ceiling
10 Safe storage of biological agents.	Yes	Yes	Yes, secure storage
11 An observation window, or alternative, is to be present, so that occupants can be seen.	No	Yes	Yes
12 A laboratory is to contain its own equipment.	No	Yes, so far as is reasonably practicable	Yes
13 Infected material, including any animal, is to be handled in a safety cabinet or isolator or other suitable containment.	Yes, where aerosol produced	Yes, where aerosol produced	Yes (Class III cabinet)
14 Incinerator for disposal of animal carcases.	Accessible	Accessible	Yes, on site

In this Part of this Schedule, "Class III cabinet" means a safety cabinet defined as such in British Standard 5726: Part I: 1992, or unit offering an equivalent level of operator protection as defined in British Standard 5726: Part I: 1992.

3, Part II

Part III Containment measures for industrial processes

Containment measures	*Containment levels* 2	3	4
1 Viable micro-organisms should be contained in a system which physically separates the process from the environment (closed system).	Yes	Yes	Yes
2 Exhaust gases from the closed system should be treated so as to -	Minimise release	Prevent release	Prevent release
3 Sample collection, addition of materials to a closed system and transfer of viable micro-organisms to another closed system, should be performed so as to -	Minimise release	Prevent release	Prevent release
4 Bulk culture fluids should not be removed from the closed system unless the viable micro-organisms have been -	Inactivated by validated means	Inactivated by validated chemical or physical means	Inactivated by validated chemical or physical means
5 Seals should be designed so as to -	Minimise release	Prevent release	Prevent release
6 Closed systems should be located within a controlled area -	Optional	Optional	Yes, and purpose-built
(a) biohazard signs should be posted;	Optional	Yes	Yes
(b) access should be restricted to nominated personnel only;	Optional	Yes	Yes, via air-lock
(c) personnel should wear protective clothing;	Yes, work clothing	Yes	Yes, a complete change
(d) decontamination and washing facilities should be provided for personnel;	Yes	Yes	Yes
(e) personnel should shower before leaving the controlled area;	No	Optional	Yes
(f) effluent from sinks and showers should be collected and inactivated before release;	No	Optional	Yes
(g) the controlled area should be adequately ventilated to minimise air contamination;	Optional	Optional	Yes
(h) the controlled area should be maintained at an air pressure negative to atmosphere;	No	Optional	Yes
(i) input and extract air to the controlled area should be HEPA filtered;	No	Optional	Yes
(j) the controlled area should be designed to contain spillage of the entire contents of closed system;	Optional	Yes	Yes
(k) the controlled area should be sealable to permit fumigation.	No	Optional	Yes
7 Effluent treatment before final discharge.	Inactivated by validated means	Inactivated by validated chemical or physical means	Inactivated by validated physical means

Schedule

3, Part IV

Part IV Biohazard sign

The biohazard sign required by paragraph 6 of Part I of this Schedule shall be in the form shown below -

Schedule

3, Part V

Part V List of biological agents referred to in paragraphs 12(2)(a), 13(1) and (3) and 14(1) of Part I of this Schedule

1 All Group 4 biological agents.

2 Rabies virus.

3 Simian herpes B virus.

4 Venezuelan equine encephalitis virus.

5 Tick-borne encephalitis group viruses in Group 3.

6 Monkeypox virus.

7 Mopeia virus.

Schedule 4

Frequency of thorough examination and test of local exhaust ventilation plant used in certain processes

Regulation 9(2)(a)

Schedule

4

Column 1 *Process*	*Column 2* *Minimum frequency*
Processes in which blasting is carried out in or incidental to the cleaning of metal castings, in connection with their manufacture.	1 month.
Processes, other than wet processes, in which metal articles (other than of gold, platinum or iridium) are ground, abraded or polished using mechanical power, in any room for more than 12 hours in any week.	6 months.
Processes giving off dust or fume in which non-ferrous metal castings are produced.	6 months.
Jute cloth manufacture.	1 month.

Schedule 5

Specific substances and processes for which monitoring is required

Regulation 10(2)

Schedule

5

Column 1 *Substance or process*	*Column 2* *Minimum frequency*
Vinyl chloride monomer.	Continuous or in accordance with a procedure approved by the Health and Safety Commission.
Spray given off from vessels at which an electrolytic chromium process is carried on, except trivalent chromium.	Every 14 days while the process is being carried on.

Medical surveillance

Regulation 11(2)(a) and (5)

Column 1 *Substances for which medical surveillance is appropriate*	*Column 2* *Process*
Vinyl chloride monomer (VCM).	In manufacture, production, reclamation, storage, discharge, transport, use or polymerisation.
Nitro or amino derivatives of phenol and of benzene or its homologues.	In the manufacture of nitro or amino derivatives of phenol and of benzene or its homologues and the making of explosives with the use of any of these substances.
Potassium or sodium chromate or dichromate.	In manufacture.
Ortho-tolidine and its salts. Dianisidine and its salts. Dichlorobenzidine and its salts.	In manufacture, formation or use of these substances.
Auramine. Magenta.	In manufacture.
Carbon disulphide. Disulphur dichloride. Benzene, including benzol. Carbon tetrachloride. Trichloroethylene.	Processes in which these substances are used, or given off as vapour, in the manufacture of indiarubber or of articles or goods made wholly or partially of indiarubber.
Pitch.	In manufacture of blocks of fuel consisting of coal, coal dust, coke or slurry with pitch as a binding substance.

Fumigations excepted from regulation 13

Regulation 13(1)

Column 1 *Fumigant*	*Column 2* *Nature of fumigation*
Hydrogen cyanide.	Fumigations carried out for research. Fumigations in fumigation chambers. Fumigations in the open air to control or kill mammal pests.
Methyl bromide.	Fumigations carried out for research. Fumigations in fumigation chambers. Fumigations of soil outdoors under gas-proof sheeting where not more than 1000 kg is used in any period of 24 hours on the premises. Fumigations of soil under gas-proof sheeting in glasshouses where not more than 500 kg is used in any period of 24 hours on the premises. Fumigations of compost outdoors under gas-proof sheeting where not more than 10 kg of methyl bromide is used in any period of 24 hours on the premises. Fumigations under gas-proof sheeting inside structures other than glasshouses and mushroom houses where not more than 5 kg of methyl bromide is used in each structure during any period of 24 hours. Fumigations of soil or compost in mushroom houses where not more than 5 kg of methyl bromide is used in any one fumigation in any period of 24 hours. Fumigations of containers where not more than 5 kg of methyl bromide is used in any one fumigation in a period of 24 hours.
Phosphine.	Fumigations carried out for research. Fumigations in fumigation chambers. Fumigations under gas-proof sheeting inside structures where not more than 1 kg of phosphine in each structure is used in any period of 24 hours. Fumigations in containers where not more than 0.5 kg of phosphine is used in any one fumigation in any period of 24 hours. Fumigations in individual impermeable packages. Fumigations in the open air to control or kill mammal pests.

Notification of certain fumigations

Regulation 13(2)

Part I Persons to whom notifications must be made

1 In the case of a fumigation to be carried out within the area of a harbour authority, advance notification of fumigation shall, for the purposes of regulation 13(2)(a), be given to -

(a) that authority;

(b) an inspector appointed under section 19 of the 1974 Act, if that inspector so requires; and

(c) where the fumigation -

(i) is to be carried out on a sea-going ship, the chief fire officer of the area in which the ship is situated and the officer in charge of the office of Her Majesty's Customs and Excise at the harbour; or

(ii) is the space fumigation of a building, the chief fire officer of the area in which the building is situated.

2 In the case of a fumigation, other than a fumigation to which paragraph (1) applies, advance notification of fumigation shall be given to -

(a) the police officer for the time being in charge of the police station for the police district in which the fumigation is carried out;

(b) an inspector appointed under section 19 of the 1974 Act, if that inspector so requires; and

(c) where the fumigation is to be carried out on a sea-going ship or is the space fumigation of a building, the chief fire officer of the area in which the ship or building is situated.

Part II Information to be given in advance notice of fumigations

3 The information to be given in a notification made for the purposes of regulation 13(2) shall include the following -

(a) the name, address and place of business of the fumigator and his telephone number;

(b) the name of the person requiring the fumigation to be carried out;

(c) the address and description of the premises where the fumigation is to be carried out;

(d) the date on which the fumigation is to be carried out and the estimated time of commencement and completion;

(e) the name of the operator in charge of the fumigation; and

(f) the fumigant to be used.

Appendix

Health records

Regulation 11(3) (General ACOP, paragraphs 91, 95 and 96)

General ACOP

Particulars approved by the Health and Safety Executive.

1 A record containing the following particulars should be kept for every employee undergoing health surveillance:

(a) surname, forenames, sex, date of birth, permanent address, postcode, National Insurance Number, date of commencement of present employment and a historical record of jobs involving exposure to substances requiring health surveillance in this employment;

(b) conclusions of all other health surveillance procedures and the date on which and by whom they were carried out. The conclusions should be expressed in terms of the employee's fitness for his work and will include, where appropriate, a record of the decisions of the employment medical adviser or appointed doctor, or conclusions of the medical practitioner, occupational health nurse or other suitably qualified or responsible person, but not confidential clinical data.

2 Where health surveillance consists only of keeping an individual health record, the particulars required are those at 1(a) above.

Health and Safety Commission

Control of carcinogenic substances

Control of Substances Hazardous to Health Regulations 1999

Approved Code of Practice

Contents

Carcinogens ACOP

Notice of Approval

By virtue of section 16(4) of the Health and Safety at Work etc Act 1974, and with the consent of the Secretary of State for the Environment, Transport and the Regions, the Health and Safety Commission has on 9 March 1999 approved this revised Code of Practice entitled *Control of carcinogenic substances* (1999 edition).

This Code of Practice gives supplementary practical guidance on the Control of Substances Hazardous to Health Regulations 1999 and should be read with the General Approved Code of Practice entitled *Control of substances hazardous to health* which comes into force on 25 March 1999.

This Code of Practice comes into effect on 25 March 1999 and on that date the edition of the Code of Practice, which came into force on 16 January 1995, shall cease to have effect.

Signed

ROSEMARY BANNER
Secretary to the Health and Safety Commission

9 March 1999

Foreword

This Code has been approved by the Health and Safety Commission and gives advice on how to comply with the law. This Code has a special legal status. If you are prosecuted for breach of health and safety law, and it is proved that you have not followed the relevant provisions of the Code, a court will find you at fault, unless you can show that you have complied with the law in some other way.

Scope of this Code

1 This Code of Practice (Carcinogens ACOP) applies where persons are exposed, or are liable to be exposed, to substances which are defined as carcinogens in the Control of Substances Hazardous to Health Regulations 1999 (COSHH) (SI 1999/437).

2 While the application of this Code depends on the potential of a substance to cause cancer, whether it does so in practice will depend on the nature and degree of exposure to it. The precautions which are required to be taken under the Regulations will be determined by the extent of the risk of cancers occurring and the scope for minimising that risk.

3 This Code is intended to give practical guidance, in relation to work involving carcinogens, on the COSHH Regulations and certain aspects of the General ACOP; it is in no way a replacement for the latter. Both Codes are concerned with the correct matching of the precautions to the risk, and should therefore be treated as complementary.

Prohibitions relating to certain substances (regulation 4)

4 The prohibited substances are listed in full in Schedule 2 to the Regulations. The following prohibitions relate to carcinogens:

(a) employment in the manufacture and use, including any process resulting in the formation, of 2-naphthylamine, benzidine, 4-aminodiphenyl, 4-nitrodiphenyl and their salts and any substance containing any of these compounds in a total concentration equal to or greater than 0.1 per cent by mass;

(b) importation of the four substances above;*

(c) use for all purposes except use in industrial processes, and for the purposes of research, development and analysis, of benzene and any other substance containing benzene in a concentration equal to or greater than 0.1 per cent by mass, other than motor fuels covered by EC Directive 85/210/EEC and waste covered by EC Directives 75/442/EEC (as amended by 91/156/EEC) and 91/689/EEC.

5 Exemption Certificates may be granted by the Health and Safety Executive under certain conditions laid down in regulation 14. Holders of Certificates of Exemption and Import Licences issued by the Health and Safety Executive under the Carcinogenic Substances Regulations 1967 and the Carcinogenic Substances (Prohibition of Importation) Order 1967 (now repealed) should have already reapplied to the Executive under regulation 14 of the Control of Substances Hazardous to Health Regulations if they wished to seek exemption from the requirements of regulation 4.

Assessment of health risks created by work involving substances hazardous to health (regulation 6)

6 The General ACOP gives guidance on assessment. Assessment has an especially vital role to play in the control of carcinogenic substances. Because

* *Note:* In April 1993, as part of the creation of the Single Market, this prohibition was removed insofar as it applied to importation from other member states of the European Community. (It has similarly been removed in respect of those non-EC countries which are, however, signatories to the Agreement on the European Economic Area, ie as defined in COSHH regulation 2(1).) In practice, however, the four substances above will not be imported. This is because the COSHH Regulations continue to prohibit their manufacture, supply and use in the UK, in line with Directive 88/364/EEC.

the development of the clinical effects of cancer may take place many years after first exposure, there may not be any early warnings of adverse effects. The assessment should identify whether substances to which this Code relates are present and, if so, the nature and extent of the risk; it should ensure that the information obtained is used to plan effective control measures and other precautions. (The Appendix gives some relevant background information.)

7 For any substance to which this Code applies, the results of assessment should at least include details of:

(a) the nature of the hazard and the nature and extent of exposure, including the identification of any workers who may be at particular risk;

(b) whether substitution by less hazardous substances is reasonably practicable;

(c) the control measures to be applied to prevent or reduce exposure and evidence that consideration has been given to not employing workers at particular risk in areas where they may be exposed to carcinogenic substances, such as pregnant women dealing with a transplacental carcinogen;

(d) operating and maintenance instructions and procedures, where relevant to ensure that exposure is minimised;

(e) precautions under non-routine conditions, including maintenance activities and emergencies;

(f) use of personal protective equipment;

(g) monitoring procedures;

(h) health surveillance procedures;

(i) arrangements for consultation with employees and their representatives, including procedures for reporting defects in plant or precautions, and details of essential information and training requirements.

8 Because it is particularly important to ensure accuracy and continuity of knowledge and action over time, the assessment and the results of the assessment should normally be recorded, where carcinogens are involved. The assessment should be reviewed:

(a) whenever there is any indication, from monitoring results or other sources of information, that standards of control have changed significantly; and

(b) within the period set in the assessment for regular automatic review, as described in the General ACOP, paragraph 26.

Prevention or control of exposure to carcinogens (regulation 7)

9 Prevention of exposure to carcinogenic substances must be the first objective, in view of the serious and often irreversible nature of the disease. Carcinogenic substances or processes should not be used or carried on where there is an equivalent but less or non-hazardous substitute. However, carcinogenic, toxic and other properties of possible chemical substitutes should be established and taken into account when considering changes. Synthetic routes for the production of chemicals should be chosen in order:

(a) to avoid the use of carcinogenic starting materials; and

(b) (together with the conditions under which substances are used) to avoid, if possible, the formation of by-products, intermediates, wastes or residual contaminants consisting of or containing carcinogenic substances.

Control of exposure (regulation 7)

10 If use of a safer alternative substance or process is not reasonably practicable, adequate control of exposure must be ensured. The General ACOP gives guidance on the meaning of 'adequate control'; in the case of carcinogens, it is particularly important that exposure should be controlled to as low a level as is reasonably practicable, bearing in mind the high risk of death associated still with many forms of cancer and the fact that the level of exposure affects only the probability of cancers occurring in any exposed population, not the severity of the disease in individuals.

11 The use of totally enclosed systems must be the first choice of control measure for carcinogens. Where this cannot be achieved, plant, processes or systems of work should be so designed and operated that they minimise the generation of, suppress and contain carcinogenic substances, for example through the partial enclosure of processes and handling systems, appropriate local exhaust ventilation systems, and general ventilation. Control measures inside the workplace must not be applied in ways which produce risks in other workplaces. Any environmental legislative requirements must also be taken into account.

12 Carcinogenic substances intended for use should be kept to the minimum needed for the process and, where appropriate, stored and transported on site in closed containers, clearly labelled and with clearly visible warning and hazard signs. There may, however, be circumstances where, to ensure the adequate control of exposure, it is preferable to store a larger quantity in a controlled manner than to deal with frequent supplies of smaller volume. Carcinogenic waste products should be clearly labelled and stored securely until such time as they are removed by a competent specialist contractor, or are disposed of safely on site by incineration or in another way that does not accentuate the risk to other workers or the outside environment.

13 The areas in which exposure to carcinogens may occur should be clearly identified and measures taken to prevent the spread of contamination within and beyond these areas. The number of people liable to be exposed to a carcinogenic substance and the duration of their exposure should be kept to the minimum necessary for the work. Non-essential personnel should be excluded.

14 Eating, drinking and smoking should not be permitted where there is a risk of contamination from the carcinogenic substance. Appropriate warning signs should be used. Areas should be set aside where people can eat, drink, and smoke without risking contamination by the substance. Appropriate hygiene measures should include the establishment of a cleaning regime to remove contamination from walls, surfaces, etc. Adequate washing facilities should be provided in order to enable people exposed to meet a standard of personal hygiene consistent with adequate control of exposure and the need to avoid the spread of carcinogenic substances.

15 If in spite of the above control measures there is an uncontrolled release of a carcinogenic substance into the place of work, means, including emergency procedures, shall be available for limiting the extent of risks to health and for regaining adequate control as soon as possible. Only those people who are essential to the carrying out of repairs and other necessary work should be permitted in the affected area.

16 In all cases, prevention or adequate control of exposure should be achieved by measures other than personal protective equipment, so far as is reasonably practicable in the light of the degree of exposure, circumstances of use, informed knowledge about its hazards and current technical developments. If the use of personal protective equipment and clothing is unavoidable, eg during a plant failure or maintenance operations, the advice in the General ACOP on its application, use and maintenance should be followed.

Monitoring exposure at the workplace (regulation 10)

17 Because exposure to carcinogens can result in a serious health effect, monitoring is normally requisite, as indicated in paragraph 72 of the General ACOP. A monitoring programme should be established and used where necessary in order to determine the extent of exposure of individuals in comparison with prescribed or approved occupational exposure limits or, if none exist, self-imposed working standards, to detect any deterioration in standards of control.

Health surveillance (regulation 11)

18 The General ACOP gives guidance on health surveillance. In the case of carcinogenic substances, some of the objectives of health surveillance and its limitations need to be emphasised.

19 Health surveillance is appropriate in the cases of all carcinogenic substances, unless exposure is not significant (see paragraph 92 of the General ACOP). Some are listed in Schedule 6 to the Regulations, as requiring medical surveillance under the supervision of an employment medical adviser or appointed doctor. In the case of substances known to, or suspected of, causing cancer of the skin (eg arsenic, coal soots, coal tar, non-solvent refined mineral oils, contaminated used mineral oils), health surveillance should include regular skin inspection by a suitably qualified person, or, alternatively, regular enquiries by a responsible person about any symptoms, following self-inspection by the employees concerned. In all other cases, only a health record, as described in paragraph 91 of the General ACOP, and paragraph 2 of the Appendix to the General ACOP, need be kept.

20 Health surveillance generally has limitations in identifying susceptible people and in the early recognition of cancer at a stage when treatment is likely to offer a better prognosis. For this reason it is largely restricted to the keeping of health records under these Regulations, in order to protect the health of workers through the detection and evaluation of risks to health. Medical surveillance by an employment medical adviser or appointed doctor is, however, required in those cases included in Schedule 6, and, in addition, skin cancer is an obvious example where appropriate health surveillance can detect the condition at an early stage when it can be cured.

21 In view of the usual latent period between exposure to a carcinogenic substance and any health effect, employees who have been exposed to carcinogenic substances should be provided with information about any need for continuing health surveillance after exposure has ceased.

Information, instruction and training for people who may be exposed to substances hazardous to health (regulation 12)

22 The General ACOP gives guidance on the provision of information, instruction and training. Because the risk of cancer from exposure to a substance cannot in most cases be presumed to be reduced to zero except by

Carcinogens ACOP

eliminating exposure and because there may be no short-term manifestation of adverse effects, it is especially important to ensure that the information, instruction and training provided is of an appropriately high standard to ensure that employees are aware of risks, including the additional risks due to tobacco consumption, and the need for control of exposure to be maintained. Where there is an uncontrolled release of a carcinogenic substance into the workplace, unless exposure is not significant, workers who may be affected must be informed of the situation as soon as possible and should have received sufficient instruction and training to ensure that emergency procedures are effective.

23 People exposed, or liable to be exposed, to carcinogenic substances, and their representatives at the workplace, should be made and kept aware of the nature of the risk, the special features of carcinogenic substances and the circumstances in which they may be exposed to carcinogenic substances, in addition to the information specified by the General ACOP.

Appendix

Background note on occupational cancer

Note: Unlike the Carcinogens Approved Code of Practice (ACOP), which has statutory force, this is general guidance and does not form part of the ACOP.

Guidance

1 Cancer is a disorder of cells in the body. It begins in a group of cells which fail to respond to the normal control mechanisms and continue to divide without need. The new growths which result are called tumours or neoplasia and may either be 'benign' or 'malignant'. A benign tumour is one which has remained localised, although it may produce adverse effects such as pressure on adjacent tissues and inhibition of their normal functions. Malignant tumours can invade and destroy neighbouring tissues, enter blood vessels, lymphatic vessels and other spaces, and can also be carried to tissues and organs elsewhere in the body to form new tumours, called 'secondaries' or 'metastases'. It is to these invasive, metastasing, malignant types of tumour that the term 'cancer' is generally applied.

2 Cancer may arise from various causes, one of which is the adverse effects of certain substances on cells in the body. The active agents can be the substances to which the body is exposed directly, or ones formed during the metabolism of those substances in the body. Certain substances do not cause cancer directly, but may promote or initiate it on exposure to additional substances or agents. Cancer does not necessarily arise in the sites of the body where exposure first occurs.

3 Such methods as exist for the assessment of the carcinogenicity of individual substances seldom give unequivocal results. Much research in recent years has, however, been directed at occupational cancer and there is now a growing number of substances to which varying degrees of suspicion are attached.

4 It may be very difficult to prove a causal link between a particular chemical and cancer in humans (though it can be very easy, as, for example, in the cases of vinyl chloride and angiosarcoma of the liver and bischloromethyl ether and cancer of the lung). The epidemiological data which would allow such a link to be established are often limited, if available at all. One major problem is simply that of collecting data on sufficient numbers of exposed individuals or cases: another is the delay between exposure and effect. In assessing the potential of a chemical substance to cause cancer in humans it is necessary to consider its chemical structure and its relationship to other known carcinogens, its metabolism and the results of laboratory and animal experiments. It is impossible to be more precise given the current state of knowledge.

5 The overall proportion of cancer which might be related to occupational exposure to substances hazardous to health is not known. A review* has suggested that 2%-6% of cancer deaths each year may be attributable to occupational hazards and a substantial number of these could be reduced if exposure to the risks was adequately controlled. (There were 159 714 cancer deaths in Britain in 1990.†) It may be difficult to identify causative agents, or to assess with accuracy the degree of risk involved at any given exposure, because:

(a) there is often a long period between exposure and effect;

* *Carcinogenic risk: getting it in proportion* Sir Richard Doll (paper in conference proceedings: Cancer in the workplace, 15 October 1992, HSE and Society of Chemical Industry).

† *Annual Abstract of Statistics 1992* (HMSO).

Guidance

(b) some types of malignant disease such as lung cancer are relatively common in the population at large, and therefore an excess incidence among people exposed to particular substances may pass undetected;

(c) histories of occupational exposure are seldom recorded;

(d) other factors such as smoking, diet, life-style or exposure to other substances or agents may act separately or synergistically with occupational factors to affect the incidence of cancer;

(e) the cause of death may not be accurately recorded on death certificates, and the changing pattern of cancer survival makes sole reliance on death certificates an inadequate indicator of true cancer incidence.

6 Even for substances identified as having the ability to cause cancer in humans the degree of risk involved in handling them varies depending on factors such as their potency, the physical form or concentration in which they are present, the manner of use and the precautions which are applied to minimise exposure. As with any type of hazardous substance the overall objective is to ensure that the risk is eliminated or reduced to extremely low levels by the adoption of control measures and other precautions which are appropriate to the nature and degree of risk in each case. The principles of occupational health, including those of occupational medicine and hygiene and the practical means by which exposure to substances hazardous to health is assessed, monitored and controlled, are no different for carcinogenic substances than for those involving other health hazards. The COSHH (Amendment) Regulations 1992 (now revoked and replaced by the COSHH Regulations 1999) introduced special provisions for prevention or control of exposure to carcinogens, but it should also be noted that many substances which are known to be carcinogenic are also likely to present additional hazards, such as acute toxicity, which also need to be controlled. Measures adequate to control toxicity, however, may not necessarily provide adequate control against cancer.

7 There are a number of important reasons which, taken together, require special attention to be given to the control of exposure to carcinogenic substances:

(a) most forms of cancer carry a high risk of premature death, although new forms of surveillance and treatment have improved the prognosis in some cases. Prevention is better than cure for all diseases; but, in the case of occupational cancer, preventing or reducing the incidence of the condition by eliminating or minimising exposure to the causative agents may be the only effective remedy;

(b) the mechanisms by which carcinogenic substances exert their effects are not fully understood and, in most cases, there are no established scientific methods by which to determine what, if any, thresholds exist below which individuals are at no risk from exposure. Thus, in the present state of knowledge it is usually not possible to specify any wholly 'safe' limits;

(c) there is commonly a long delay, sometimes decades, between first exposure and the occurrence of cancer. As a consequence of this 'latent period' there is no short-term indication that a particular person exposed to carcinogenic substances is being adversely affected;

(d) cancer is more feared than most other causes of death, because of the association with pain and the uncertainty of the period between diagnosis and the outcome of treatment.

Appendix

Guidance

8 This Code deals with those defined* specific substances and processes with which a cancer hazard is associated. This does not imply that all other substances or processes present no cancer hazard or that appropriate precautions are not necessary where this Code does not apply. Medical research continues to discover further substances and processes to which varying degrees of suspicion of causing cancer are attached. These include substances classified as a carcinogen Category 3; R40 ('possible risk of irreversible effects') under the Chemicals (Hazard Information and Packaging for Supply) Regulations 1994 (as amended). For these substances and processes, HSE recommends a precautionary policy of prevention and control based on up-to-date knowledge of the substance suspected of being carcinogenic but not defined as a carcinogen under COSHH. This policy is set out in paragraph 2 of the General ACOP.

9 This background note addresses occupational cancer, but these are not the only hazards of cancer that are likely to be encountered during the working day. They constitute only a small proportion of the total risk of cancer (see table below). Industry can help to reduce the total risk by ensuring that workers have an opportunity to work not only where the risks from defined specific industrial carcinogens are prevented or adequately controlled, but where they can also work in an atmosphere free from tobacco smoke (smoking is responsible for some 33% of all deaths from cancer and about a quarter of all cases of lung cancer in non-smokers are attributable to environmental tobacco smoke (Wald et al, 1986))** and from high concentrations of natural radon (radon is estimated to cause about 6% of all lung cancers, mostly in synergism with smoking)† and that, when they take meals at work they have an opportunity of eating foods that will help to reduce rather than increase the risk of cancer.‡

Proportion of cancer deaths attributable to different factors (modified from Doll and Peto, 1981)

	Per cent of cancer deaths	
Factor	*certain*	*possible* §
Tobacco	33	35
Diet	10	60
Natural radiation (sunlight, radon, etc)	4	4
Alcohol	3	4
Natural hormones	2	20
Occupation	2	6
Viruses	2	5
Pollution and industrial products	<1	5
Medicines and medical procedures	<1	1
Other and unknown	0	?

* Regulation 2 of COSHH
** *Passive smoking at work* INDG63(rev1) revised HSE leaflet
† *Radon in the workplace* INDG210 HSE leaflet
‡ *Nutritional aspects of the development of cancer* Health Education Authority ISBN 0 7521 1100 0
§ The percentages of 'possibles' add up to more than 100% because the influences of some 'causes' may be combined with other causes (eg radon and smoking).

Appendix

Health and Safety Commission

Control of biological agents

Control of Substances Hazardous to Health Regulations 1999

Approved Code of Practice

Contents

Biological agents ACOP

Notice of Approval

By virtue of section 16(4) of the Health and Safety at Work etc Act 1974, and with the consent of the Secretary of State for the Environment, Transport and the Regions, the Health and Safety Commission has on 9 March 1999 approved this revised Code of Practice entitled *Control of biological agents* (1999 edition).

This Code of Practice gives supplementary practical guidance on the Control of Substances Hazardous to Health Regulations 1999 and should be read with the General Approved Code of Practice entitled *Control of substances hazardous to health* which comes into force on 25 March 1999.

This Code of Practice comes into effect on 25 March 1999 and on that date the edition of the Code of Practice, which came into force on 16 January 1995, shall cease to have effect.

Signed

ROSEMARY BANNER
Secretary to the Health and Safety Commission

9 March 1999

Foreword

This Code has been approved by the Health and Safety Commission and gives advice on how to comply with the law. This Code has a special legal status. If you are prosecuted for breach of health and safety law, and it is proved that you have not followed the relevant provisions of the Code, a court will find you at fault, unless you can show that you have complied with the law in some other way.

Scope of this Code

1 This Code of Practice (Biological agents ACOP) applies where people are exposed, or are liable to be exposed, to anything defined as a biological agent in the Control of Substances Hazardous to Health Regulations 1999 (COSHH) (SI 1999/437).

2 The precautions that have to be taken under the Regulations, and the detailed application of this Code, will be determined by the risk of harm and the scope for reducing it. Key elements of the risk are the potential of a biological agent to cause harm and the nature and degree of exposure to it.

3 The Code is intended to give practical guidance on the COSHH Regulations and certain aspects of the General ACOP, in relation to work involving biological agents. It does not replace the General ACOP but adds to its guidance dealing with the special features of biological agents. The two Codes are complementary and should be used together.

Definitions and classification (regulation 2 and Schedule 3, paragraphs 1 and 3)

4 The definition of 'biological agent' includes the general class of micro-organisms, and also cell cultures and human endoparasites, provided that they have one or more of the harmful properties specified in the definition. Most biological agents are micro-organisms, among which are bacteria, viruses, fungi, microscopic parasites (such as malarial parasites, amoebae and trypanosomes) and the microscopic infectious forms of larger parasites (eg the microscopic ova and infectious larval forms of helminths pathogenic to humans). Naked DNA is not a biological agent.

5 Biological agents are classified into four hazard groups according to their ability to cause *infection*, the severity of the disease that may result, the risk that infection will spread to the community, and the availability of vaccines and effective treatment. These infection criteria are the *only* ones used for classification purposes, even though an infectious biological agent may have toxic, allergenic or other harmful properties, and some biological agents are not infectious at all. A non-infectious biological agent falls into Group l; substantial control measures may still be needed for it, depending on the other harmful properties it has.

6 Any biological agent which appears in a classification list approved by the Health and Safety Commission (referred to as an 'approved classification') falls into the hazard group specified there. However, where a strain is attenuated or has lost virulence as a result of genetic modification it may in effect be reclassified by the employer, using the criteria in Schedule 3, paragraph 3, for the purpose of selecting containment measures under Schedule 3, paragraphs 7 and 8. In other words, it may be treated as though it were a different agent from the parent that appears in an approved classification. Conversely, an agent modified in such a way that it becomes more hazardous may need to be regarded as though it appeared in a higher hazard group than the parent.

7 An approved classification is not exhaustive and a biological agent that does not appear in one does *not* automatically fall into Group 1. The correct group for an unlisted agent must be determined by the employer, applying the infection criteria in Schedule 3, paragraph 3 and taking into account the relevant factors used in making the risk assessment required by COSHH regulation 6 (see also paragraphs 8-13 of this Code). If the agent subsequently appears in a later edition of an approved classification, the classification given to it in that edition takes priority.

Biological agents ACOP

Assessment of health risks created by work involving biological agents (regulation 6 and Schedule 3, paragraph 4)

8 The General ACOP gives guidance on assessment. For biological agents, as distinct from other substances hazardous to health, the assessment should reflect the ability they may have to replicate and infect. In general, there will not be a dose-response relationship of the kind that exists for many other substances, and risk may be high at small exposures. Relevant information on the nature of a particular agent includes that prepared by the Advisory Committee on Dangerous Pathogens.

9 Where parts of the assessment required by COSHH regulation 6 have already been made to meet the requirements of the Genetically Modified Organisms (Contained Use) Regulations or the Genetically Modified Organisms (Deliberate Release) Regulations, they need not be repeated.

10 Three broad categories of exposure to biological agents may be distinguished:

(i) exposure which does not arise out of the work activity itself, for example where an employee catches a respiratory infection from another;

(ii) exposure which does arise out of the work activity but is incidental to it; the activity does not involve direct work with or the use of the agent itself. Examples of activities in which there may be exposure of this kind are food production, agriculture, refuse disposal and work in sewage purification and health care;

(iii) exposure resulting from a deliberate intention to use or work with a biological agent.

The COSHH Regulations do not apply to exposure in the first of these categories. A suitable and sufficient assessment should always be made for the other two, though the scope for risk reduction and the range of applicable control measures, and therefore the level of detail required in the assessment, may be less for an activity in category (ii) than for one in category (iii).

11 In medical and veterinary care facilities, and, for example, livestock farming and slaughter-house work, the assessment should take account of uncertainties about the presence of infectious agents in patients or animals. The risks associated with tissues and other waste material removed from patients and animals, or specimens sent for examination, should be assessed at each stage of handling: for example, during clinical care, surgery, biopsy and other specimen collection, specimen handling and transportation, laboratory examination and waste disposal.

12 Subject to paragraphs 10 and 11 of this ACOP, an assessment for biological agents should include consideration of:

(a) the biological agents that may be present;

(b) what hazard groups they belong to;

(c) what form they are in (see also paragraph 13(a) of this ACOP);

(d) the diseases they may cause;

(e) how and where they are present and how they are transmitted;

(f) the likelihood of exposure and consequent disease (including the identification of workers who may be particularly susceptible, for example because they are immuno-compromised), drawing on evidence of the prevalence of infection or other ill effect as experienced within a particular industry sector or workplace;

(g) whether the nature of the activity will permit substitution by a less hazardous agent;

(h) the control measures to be applied, and minimisation of the number of people exposed;

(i) the need for monitoring procedures;

(j) the need for health surveillance procedures.

13 In considering the agent itself and its effects, the assessor should take the following into account:

(a) the forms in which the agent may appear, including the possibility that it may form hardy spores or cysts that may be resistant to disinfection, or go through a developmental cycle in which there are non-infectious forms or dependence on an intermediate host;

(b) the possible presence of 'passenger' or contaminant viruses or other agents in otherwise non-hazardous cell cultures;

(c) the possibility that cells derived from tumours, or cells rendered immortal, may be capable of colonising an exposed person following accidental innoculation; or that cells may produce high levels of hazardous proteins;

(d) that it may be necessary to assume the presence of agents as yet unidentified, for example those assumed to be associated with the transmissible spongiform encephalopathies.

Prevention or control of exposure to biological agents (regulation 7 and Schedule 3, paragraphs 5 and 6)

14 Paragraphs 5 and 6 of Schedule 3 should be read together with regulation 7. Their combined effect is as follows:

(a) exposure to a particular biological agent should be prevented if this is reasonably practicable. Among the methods to be considered (see General ACOP paragraph 30) are any ways that exist of carrying out the activity without involving a biological agent at all;

(b) then, if it is not reasonably practicable to prevent exposure to all biological agents, the biological agent involved in the activity should be the least harmful that the nature of the activity will permit. Often there will be no choice, especially where exposure is incidental (paragraph 10(ii) of this ACOP), but some selection may be possible, for example in teaching and some types of research.

15 Any exposure there is to a biological agent after these steps have been taken should be adequately controlled. Biological agents are not among the substances covered by regulation 7(2) and all of the measures listed in Schedule 3, paragraph 6 should be considered. Each should be used where and to the extent that:

(a) it is applicable; *and*

(b) the assessment carried out under regulation 6 shows that it will lead to a reduction in risk.

16 The selection of control measures for biological agents should take into account the fact that there are no exposure limits for them. Their ability to replicate and to infect at very small doses means that exposure may have to be reduced to levels that are at the limit of detection.

17 *Not all the listed measures will be required in every case.* The assessment may indicate for example that a specific mode of transmission and route of infection is required, a susceptible host is needed, there is a low prevalence of the infection in that particular activity, and that illness is easily treatable leading to rapid and complete recovery. In such a case the risk would be relatively low and the control measures required less stringent. Another factor that will determine which controls are to be applied may be the extent to which the activity involves the handling or deliberate use of a biological agent, or exposure is incidental to the main purpose of the work (see also paragraph 10(ii) of this ACOP). But the level of risk should be the principal consideration, and even where exposure is incidental to the activity, if the risk is sufficiently high and some of the listed measures can reduce it, then those measures should be applied.

Health and veterinary care, laboratories, animal rooms and industrial processes (Schedule 3, paragraphs 7 and 8)

18 Certain special measures are required in health and veterinary care facilities (for example hospitals, surgeries and clinics), laboratories, animal rooms and industrial processes that involve the use of biological agents, to ensure that biological agents are not transmitted to workers or outside the controlled area. For laboratories, animal rooms and industrial processes, rules are laid down for the derivation of containment level from the hazard classification of the agent, or from what is suspected about the possible presence of an agent. In particular:

(a) laboratories which handle materials in which there is reason to suppose that agents in Group 2 or above may be present, though their presence is not intrinsic to the activity, should achieve containment level 2 as a minimum (Schedule 3, paragraph 8(4)(d)). This means that laboratories screening for an agent that falls into Group 3, say, but which is not ordinarily expected to be present (for example a microbiological laboratory in a food factory screening for salmonella, with the possibility of finding *Salmonella typhi*), should work at level 2 but switch to the appropriate higher level if the agent is found and if work is to continue with it;

(b) Schedule 3, paragraph 8(4)(e) requires that in a laboratory that does not deliberately work with biological agents, but the presence of agents calling for containment levels 3 or 4 is nevertheless known or suspected, then those containment levels should be used, *unless* guidance issued by HSE makes it clear that a lower level is permissible. Guidance may indicate, for example, that in serology, clinical chemistry, haematology or forensic science laboratories where materials liable to be contaminated with a particular Group 3 virus are handled, uprated level 2 containment may nevertheless be used. Employers should be sure of the scope and meaning of guidance before making a decision to use a lower level of containment on the basis of it, and if in doubt should consult HSE.

Agents with reduced virulence may also be used at a lower than normal level of containment if the alteration has effectively changed their classification (see paragraph 6 of this ACOP).

19 A biological agent that falls or is treated as falling into Hazard Group 1 may be a Group II GMO, as defined in the Genetically Modified Organisms (Contained Use) Regulations, because of environmental risks associated with it. Where there is a mismatch of this kind, the more stringent requirements should be followed.

20 Where the rules set out in Schedule 3, paragraphs 7 and 8 lead to a particular containment level for an activity, all the measures appropriate to that level should normally be considered (noting that measures additional to those listed in Parts II and III of Schedule 3 may be necessary in particular cases). Some selection may be done, however, to suit individual circumstances, provided that by doing so risk is not increased. Very small-scale industrial processes, for example, may not require all the measures set out in Schedule 3, Part III which are appropriate to large-scale activity, but assessment may show that additional measures of a laboratory type are necessary. It may be possible to achieve separation of such processes from the environment by means of a suitable safety cabinet for example, or by other forms of primary containment. Where human patients or animals infected with agents in Group 3 or Group 4 are to be accommodated in isolation facilities, the measures taken should be selected from the first column of Part II of Schedule 3. The choice should be on the basis of risk assessment and in particular the nature of the infection and the facility for and mode of transmission of the agent.

Maintenance, examination and test of protective clothing and equipment (regulation 9 and Schedule 3, paragraph 9)

21 Schedule 3, paragraph 9 sets out additional requirements in respect of personal protective equipment used to protect workers against biological agents. The object of these requirements is to prevent the equipment itself from acting as the means by which agents are transmitted, and they should be followed accordingly.

Monitoring exposure at the workplace (regulation 10)

22 The routine use of atmospheric and personal sampling methods to obtain a quantitive estimate of exposure is not normally appropriate to biological agents and is therefore not 'requisite' under regulation 10. Where a suitable technique is available, however, and the information obtained can be acted upon in the maintenance of adequate control or the protection of workers' health, testing for the presence of an agent outside the primary physical confinement should be carried out. The integrity of industrial process systems (for example filters, seals, or pipework joints) may be tested by swabbing and air sampling provided that methods are standardised, sufficiently sensitive and of proven effectiveness, but wherever possible such testing should be done using harmless surrogate organisms whose release under test conditions mimics the release of process organisms.

Health surveillance (regulation 11)

23 The General ACOP gives guidance on health surveillance. One objective of health surveillance in relation to biological agents is to assess employees' immunity, for example before or after vaccination, but routine testing for antibody or the taking of specimens to attempt to isolate infectious agents is not generally appropriate until there is an indication that infection may have occurred. If an employee is found to be suffering from an infection or illness

which is suspected to be the result of exposure at work, other employees who have been similarly exposed should be placed under suitable surveillance until it is established that they are not affected. Where there are early symptoms of disease that employees themselves may be able to recognise, an effective measure is to provide instruction and information that will enable them to do so, and systems for symptom reporting, though this is not 'health surveillance' within the strict meaning of the Regulations.

24 Susceptibility to microbial allergens is not predictable, but when an allergy develops it may be possible to show by immunological testing which agents are responsible. Where there is evidence of sensitisation in an individual, health surveillance of that person should be carried out if it can be demonstrated that it is associated with the work.

25 Where workers are known to be exposed to respiratory sensitisers of biological origin, all should be under surveillance unless assessment shows that there is unlikely to be a risk under the conditions of the work. The level of surveillance should be related to the degree of risk identified.

Information for people who may be exposed to biological agents (regulation 12 and Schedule 3, paragraph 10)

26 Schedule 3, paragraph 10 requires that where workers are exposed to biological agents the information and instruction given to them on the following subjects under COSHH regulation 12, if applicable, should be set down in the form of written instructions:

(a) the procedure to be followed after an accident or incident which may have resulted or actually did result in the release of a biological agent with the potential to cause severe human disease;

(b) the procedure for handling any Group 4 agent.

If the nature of the workplace and the activity are such that workers may need instant access to this information, or where a reduction in risk may be expected by having the information conspicuously and constantly before the eye, then it should also be set out on notices displayed in the workplace. Schedule 3, paragraph 10 deals solely with the subjects in (a) and (b), and does not imply that other information and instruction given under regulation 12 need not be put in writing.

List of employees exposed to certain biological agents (Schedule 3, paragraph 11)

27 The list required by Schedule 3, paragraph 11 is not the same as a health record kept in accordance with regulation 11. It need be kept only where there is a deliberate intention to work with or use a Group 3 or 4 agent (see paragraph 10 of this ACOP), unless in a case of incidental exposure the assessment carried out in accordance with regulation 6 shows that there is significant risk. The risk should be taken as significant if it is such that more than basic hygiene is needed to deal with it, that is, if the employer has to take specific and deliberate action to apply the control measures set out in Schedule 3, paragraph 6. For example, the risk may not be significant in food processing, but will probably be so in an isolation unit for the accommodation of patients or animals with Group 3 or 4 infections. Employees should be counted as having been exposed unless exposure has been *prevented* and not merely controlled (see General ACOP, paragraph 30).

Notification of the use or storage of biological agents (Schedule 3, paragraph 12)

28 Schedule 3, paragraph 12 requires that certain activities involving biological agents should be notified to HSE, unless notification has already been made under the Genetically Modified Organisms (Contained Use) Regulations. Notice must be given:

(a) of an intention to use or store an agent or agents from a particular *group*, other than Group 1, **for the first time**. Only the group need normally be notified, but the actual agents to be used or stored at the time of this first involvement with a group should also be identified:

  (i) if they are among those specified in Part V of Schedule 3. It should be noted that this includes all Group 4 agents whether or not they appear in an approved classification;

  (ii) if they are Group 3 agents which do not appear in an approved classification;

(b) subsequently, of the use or storage for the first time of:

  (i) any particular Part V agent not already notified, whether or not it appears in an approved classification; and

  (ii) any Group 3 agent that does not appear in an approved classification.

If a notification under (a) has specified all Part V or Group 4 agents in the approved classification, then the requirement to notify in respect of those agents under (b)(i) will vanish.

29 The term 'use' in Schedule 3, paragraph 12 should be taken to exclude activities in which agents are incidentally present (see paragraph 10 of this ACOP), but to include the provision of a diagnostic service.

30 However there are derogations from the duty to notify where the activity is the provision of a diagnostic service:

(a) the duty described in paragraph 28(a) of this ACOP does not apply to the provision of a diagnostic service for Group 2 agents, or for Group 3 agents except for those that are included in Part V, unless a process likely to propagate or concentrate an agent is involved. In general this will relieve, for example, haematology, clinical chemistry or histopathology laboratories providing diagnostic support in the care of Group 2 or 3 infected patients from the duty to notify in respect of those activities. Laboratories providing any kind of diagnostic service in relation to Part V agents are subject to the duty in full;

(b) the duty described in paragraph 28(b) of this ACOP does not apply to the provision of a diagnostic service unless a process likely to propagate or concentrate an agent is involved, and the agent does not appear in an approved classification.

Notification of the consignment of biological agents (Schedule 3, paragraph 13)

31 Schedule 3, paragraph 13 requires that notification is given to HSE when

Biological agents ACOP

a biological agent or anything known or suspected of containing it is consigned to other premises, if:

(a) the agent appears in Part V of Schedule 3;

(b) the consignment is not for the purpose of diagnosis or disposal, or the medical treatment of a human or other animal.

A single set of premises may include more than one building, and transportation from one to another in such a case is not notifiable.

Printed and published by the Health and Safety Executive C50 7/00